Two Parties—Or More?
Second Edition

Dilemmas in American Politics

Series Editor: **L. Sandy Maisel,** Colby College

If the answers to the problems facing American democracy were easy, politicians would solve them, accept credit, and move on. But, certain dilemmas have confronted the American political system continuously. They defy solution; they are endemic to the system. Some can best be described as institutional dilemmas: How can the Congress be both a representative body and a national decision maker? How can the President communicate with over 250 million citizens effectively? Why do we have a two-party system when many voters are disappointed with the choices presented to them? Others are policy dilemmas: How do we find compromises on issues that defy compromise, such as abortion policy? How do incorporate racial and ethnic minorities or immigrant groups into American society, allowing them to reap the benefits of this land without losing their identity? How do we fund health care for our poorest or oldest citizens?

Dilemmas such as these are what propel students toward an interest in the study of American government. Each book in the *Dilemmas in American Politics Series* addresses a "real world" problem, raising the issues that are of most concern to students. Each is structured to cover the historical and theoretical aspects of the dilemma, but also to explore the dilemma from a practical point of view and to speculate about the future. The books are designed as supplements to introductory courses in American politics or as case studies to be used in upper level courses. The link among them is the desire to make the real issues confronting the political world come alive in students' eyes.

BOOKS IN THIS SERIES

Two Parties—Or More? The American Party System, Second Edition,
John F. Bibby and L. Sandy Maisel

*"Can We All Get Along?" Racial and Ethnic Minorities in
American Politics, Third Edition,* Paula D. McClain and Joseph Stewart Jr.

*The Role of the Supreme Court in American Politics:
The Least Dangerous Branch?,* Richard L. Pacelle Jr.

*The New Citizenship: Unconventional Politics, Activism,
and Service, Second Edition,* Craig A. Rimmerman

*Onward Christian Soldiers? The Religious Right in
American Politics, Second Edition,* Clyde Wilcox

*To Serve God and Mammon: Church-State
Relations in American Politics,* Ted Jelen

Money Rules: Financing Elections in America,
Anthony Gierzynski

*The Dysfunctional Congress? The Individual Roots of an
Institutional Dilemma,* Kenneth R. Mayer and David T. Canon

The Accidental System: Health Care Policy in America,
Michael D. Reagan

The Image-Is-Everything Presidency: Dilemma in American Leadership,
Richard W. Waterman, Robert Wright, and Gilbert St. Clair

*The Angry American: How Voter Rage Is Changing the
Nation, Second Edition,* Susan J. Tolchin

*Remote and Controlled: Media Politics in a Cynical Age,
Second Edition,* Matthew Robert Kerbel

*Checks and Balances? How a Parliamentary System Could Change
American Politics,* Paul Christopher Manuel and Anne Marie Cammisa

*Making Americans, Remaking America: Immigration and
Immigrant Policy,* Louis DeSipio and Rodolfo de la Garza

From Rhetoric to Reform? Welfare Policy in American Politics,
Anne Marie Cammisa

No Neutral Ground? Abortion Politics in an Age of Absolutes,
Karen O'Connor

Payment Due: A Nation in Debt, a Generation in Trouble,
Timothy J. Penny and Steven E. Schier

Bucking the Deficit: Economic Policymaking in the United States,
G. Calvin Mackenzie and Saranna Thornton

Two Parties —Or More?

The American Party System, Second Edition

John F. Bibby
University of Wisconsin, Milwaukee

L. Sandy Maisel
Colby College

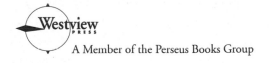
A Member of the Perseus Books Group

Dilemmas in American Politics

Copyright © 2003, 1998 by Westview Press, A Member of the Perseus Books Group

Westview Press books are available at special discounts for bulk purchases in the United States by corporations, institutions, and other organizations. For more information, please contact the Special Markets Department at the Perseus Books Group, 11 Cambridge Center, Cambridge MA 02142, or call (617) 252-5298.

Published in 2003 in the United States of America by Westview Press, 5500 Central Avenue, Boulder, Colorado 80301–2877, and in the United Kingdom by Westview Press, 12 Hid's Copse Road, Cumnor Hill, Oxford OX2 9JJ

Library of Congress Cataloging-in-Publication Data

Bibby, John F.
    Two parties-or more? : the American party system / John F. Bibby and L. Sandy Maisel.— 2nd ed.
        p.   cm. — (Dilemmas in American politics)
Includes bibliographical references and index.
    ISBN 0-8133-4030-6 (hc : alk. paper) — ISBN 0-8133-4031-4 (pbk : alk. paper)
    1. Political parties—United States—History. 2. Third parties (United States politics)—History. I. Maisel, Louis Sandy, 1945– II. Title. III. Series.
JK2261 .B493 2002
324.273—dc21

                                                                      2002005027

The paper used in this publication meets the requirements of the American National Standard for Permanence of Paper for Printed Library Materials Z39.48–1984.

10   9   8   7   6   5   4   3   2   1

To Lucile from John
To Patrice from Sandy

Contents

Tables and Figures

Tables

Figures

Preface and Acknowledgments

AT TIMES ONE WONDERS what purpose an Editorial Board serves for a series such as this. For this series, this volume answers that question. We both have served on the Editorial Board for the Dilemmas in American Politics Series since its inception; Sandy Maisel is the series editor, and John Bibby was one of the first scholars he recruited to work with him. By design, the board is composed of leading scholars who have demonstrated an interest in undergraduate education. The goal of the series is to publish high-quality books that will stimulate student interest in introductory courses, to produce supplementary texts that will provide a "real-world" context for the more theoretical material often presented in such courses. The board's role has been to set the direction that the series will take.

The genesis of this book was an Editorial Board meeting at which potential topics for Dilemmas books were discussed. After listing subjects that would be important additions to introductory courses in American government and politics, the board turned to the more difficult task—suggesting potential authors for the books that were proposed. At this stage the question is always twofold: Who would be a good author to add to the series? Who would be available to write a Dilemmas book in a relatively short period of time?

For each potential topic, several authors were suggested. When the discussion turned to a book on the party system, a topic that had been mentioned at previous meetings but for which no suitable author had been found, the board became strangely silent. Finally, one of our colleagues turned to us and said, "Well, are you guys going to do it or not?" And thus our discussion began.

Of course, our first response to the suggestion was to think of the reasons we should not write this book. The series editor is in a somewhat compromised position if he is also an author: How can he appraise his own work objectively, especially when he is writing with another member of the board? Although we have known each other for more than two decades, we have never worked together on a scholarly project: Was a book of this sort the place to begin? We both had other publishing commitments: Would we have time to give this project its due?

But the reasons the project was intriguing to us were also apparent. This topic was one that we had both been thinking about for many years. Despite the fact that we have been party activists—one as a Republican, one as a Democrat—

throughout our careers, we share the views that are presented in this book. Specifically, as you will see, we believe that those who favor the advent of a third major party in the American system or those who advocate more independent candidacies misjudge the causes of discontent with two-party politics and underestimate both the positive attributes of our two-party system and the inevitable negative consequences of a multiparty system, or worse still, they discount the adverse impact of victories by antiparty independents. These views are not de rigueur, to be sure; thus we feel they are particularly important for undergraduates to confront.

Furthermore, we thought that it might be fun to work together. Testing out one's ideas on a colleague who shares a substantive interest is always a good experience. We both felt that our ideas would sharpen and our own work improve because of this endeavor. We also quickly found that our work styles were compatible. This book is synthetic in nature, that is, it involved a great deal of thinking and discussing of topics but little new research. We decided we would only undertake it if we could complete the task over one summer—and only if we could do it while still finding time to chase that infuriating little ball around various golf courses. Now that is compatibility!

Thus, we present here our best thinking about why the two-party system in the United States has existed and should continue to exist. We know that many who will read this volume will not come to it with that predilection. We hope that grappling with the ideas in this book, coming to understand what has indeed been an enduring dilemma in American politics, will encourage students to think more deeply about how our system of government and politics works—and how they would like it to work.

Authors accumulate many debts in completing a book such as this. We would like to acknowledge the important contribution made by the members of the Dilemmas in American Politics Editorial Board, particularly Ruth Jones, who read the entire manuscript, provided the title, helped us to retain our focus, and even edited our prose. We would also like to thank Leo Wiegman, our editor at Westview Press for the first edition of this book, and his assistant, Adina Popescu. We also want to thank Steve Catalano, who has been the editor as this second edition has been produced.

Dawn DiBlasi, secretary to the Department of Government at Colby College, typed portions of the original manuscript as we dealt with two seemingly incompatible computer systems. Kendra Ammann, Alex Quigley, and Rebecca Ryan not only helped Maisel as research assistants but also read all of the manuscript with the careful eyes of students alert to what their peers look for in a text. We thank them all for their talents and efforts. For the second edition, Maisel thanks Brooke McNally, Oliver Sabot, and Kim Victor for their most effective and efficient work as research assistants. He is particularly grateful to Brooke, who managed the transition of material from the first edition to this one.

Finally, we dedicate this book to our wives. Each is an educator and has helped us incalculably as we have developed our own skills. Although our wives have never met each other—and neither of us met the other's wife until after the first edition was completed—we both have seen as we have worked on this project how they each play the primary support role in our lives. This dedication is merely a small token to express how fortunate we are to have them as our partners.

John F. Bibby
L. Sandy Maisel

1

···

Third Parties in American Politics

Eugene V. Debs, the 1912 presidential nominee of the Socialist party, won six percent of the popular vote. This was the party's greatest showing of electoral strength.

CITIZENS WERE NOT HAPPY with the choice between the Democratic candidate, Vice President Al Gore, and the Republican candidate, Texas governor George W. Bush, in the 2000 presidential election. Fewer than 50 percent of those eligible to vote bothered to turn up at the polls. According to a Shorenstein Center poll taken in December 1998, 45 percent of those polled expressed dissatisfaction with the two major party candidates and wanted a third alternative. But fewer than 5 percent of the voters chose any of the alternative party candidates running less than two years later. The showing of the Reform party, founded by Ross Perot, was so poor that it lost the federal funding it had achieved in the 1996 election. Ralph Nader's Green party did not reach the 5 percent threshold necessary for federal funding in 2004, one of its stated goals.

American electoral politics have been dominated by two major parties for virtually all of this nation's existence. Since the formation of the Republican party and the demise of the Whigs nearly a century and a half ago, either the Republicans or the Democrats have won every presidential election and controlled both houses of the U.S. Congress. Every state legislature except that of Nebraska, which is unique in that it has a **unicameral, nonpartisan** state legislature, is controlled by either the Democratic or the Republican party—and the other party is the only contender for power. Forty-eight of the fifty state governors serving in 2000 won election as either a Democrat or a Republican; Maine's Angus King, an **independent who ran without any party label**, and Minnesota's Jesse Ventura, who ran as a Reform party candidate but later left that organization, are the only exceptions.

But two-party politics is not written into the Constitution or into the laws of the land. Non-major party candidates have drawn serious media and voter attention in four of the six most recent presidential elections. In the 1992 election, Ross Perot led in the public opinion polls as late as only five months before the election, according to Gallup surveys; he eventually received approximately 20 percent of the vote, more than any non-major party candidate since former president Theodore Roosevelt bolted his Republican party to run in 1912 on the ticket of the Bull Moose Progressive party. In the 1990s, Republican and Democratic candidates for governor were beaten not only by King in Maine and Ventura in Minnesota but also by Lowell Weicker in Connecticut and Walter Hickel in

Alaska, and media polling has consistently shown that voters express a distaste for the major parties and a longing for a "third-party" alternative (Collet, 1996a).

Thus, students of American politics have been faced with an enduring dilemma: Why two major parties—and not more? Why has the **two-party system**, with few variations, remained in place in almost every jurisdiction in this country since the original parties were formed nearly 200 years ago? Although other democracies around the world support the multiparty system, why have minor parties come and gone in American politics, always to leave two-party domina tion as our political modus operandi?

This dilemma has both an empirical and a normative dimension. First, students of elections in the United States need to be aware of why this pattern has persisted. What is it about the political context in this country, about the system of government, and about the laws that are in place that supports a two-party system and discourages the growth and persistence of additional parties? Despite an antiparty heritage from our founders and repeated expression of dissatisfaction with the two parties in place, why has the two-party system remained?

Perhaps more important—and more controversial—is the second dimension of the dilemma: Is the two-party system good or bad for the United States? Should those who are concerned about the health of this democracy seek changes that would encourage the growth and increased success of additional parties and their candidates? What would be the consequences of a three- or a multiparty system for the functioning of American democracy? Before one can begin to answer these questions, it is important to understand the role that political parties play in any democratic system of government.

Political parties are organizations that serve to link the general public to those who are in government. In the classic Athenian democracy, every citizen (of course, the Athenians had a very restrictive definition of "citizenship") participated directly in making governmental decisions. In small towns in New England today, decisions are often made in town meetings, in which every citizen has a right to participate. But in a polity as large as the United States, all citizens cannot have their views heard directly. Parties bring scattered elements of the public together and define basic principles that unite them. They then work to elect public officials who will implement policies that reflect those principles.

Political parties are thus intermediaries between the citizens and the government. If they function well, they make it easier for citizens' views to be converted into public policy. Various scholars have categorized the specific means that political parties use to perform this role. They aggregate the opinions and interests of different elements of society; they socialize new citizens into the political system; they recruit leaders to serve in the government; they compromise among competing demands among their followers; they contest elections that in turn legitimize the power of those in government; and they organize the government. To be sure, political parties are not the only organizations in democracies that perform these intermediating functions. Interest groups and the mass media are two others that come quickly to mind. But the role of parties is unique in that they structure the contest for office. Political parties nominate candidates for offices at all levels throughout the land; candidates run under those party labels; and citizens who support the political parties evaluate those candidates, in part at least, because of their affiliation with the political parties (see Bibby, 2000:7–18; Maisel, 2001:13–22).

Political parties make a particularly important contribution to citizen control of government. American government is incredibly complex, with a wide array of issues and many candidates for various offices at the national, state, and local levels. Even the most conscientious citizens can be overwhelmed while trying to become well informed before casting their votes on election day. Fortunately, voters can respond to the multitude of issues and candidates in terms of a few simple criteria and are not required to spend all of their available time studying politics.

Party labels enable voters to sort out the complexity of American politics by allowing them to vote for the candidates of their preferred party—the party that they believe is closer to their interests and beliefs. And because major elected officials all wear a party label, voters can also assign to the party in power either credit or, more likely, blame for the state of the union. Without party labels to help sort out and make sense of the issues and candidates, the average voter would be at sea with no compass for a guide in making election day choices. Periodic elections that utilize party labels thus give the voters a chance to register their reaction to a party's stewardship in office. Thus, Presidents Ronald Reagan and Bill Clinton were rewarded with new four-year leases on the White House in 1984 and 1996, respectively, whereas Presidents Jimmy Carter (1980) and George Bush (1992) were forced to vacate 1600 Pennsylvania Avenue after only one term. Because voters can use party labels to assign credit and blame for government performance, political parties provide an essential means of making elected officials accountable to the citizens.

This discussion of the role of political parties implies the notion of a party system. In a democracy, if parties are to structure the contest for office, they must take each other into account. Party systems are characterized on two different axes. First, they differ from each other in terms of the number of parties effectively contesting for office. The American national system is a two-party system because only the Republicans and the Democrats are thought to have legitimate chances of victory in national elections. In countries with multiparty systems, more than two parties must take each other into account as they set strategies and appeal to the electorate. Party systems also differ in terms of the degree to which elections are competitive. For much of the twentieth century, the American South was not competitive, in that only Democrats had a real chance of winning. Nationally, however, the American system is generally classified as a competitive two-party system.

Few would argue that electoral competition is not beneficial in a democracy. But arguments certainly exist over whether a two-party system is preferable to a three- or a multiparty system. American citizens must reach a consensus on which aspects of our representative democracy are most important. How should interests be aggregated? Should they be aggregated more broadly, under the umbrellas of only two parties, with a great deal of compromise necessary to accommodate a range of interests within each party? Or should they be aggregated more narrowly, with more parties defining more specific policy alternatives, but with less room for compromise? Certainly, among the most important criteria one would use in evaluating a democracy would be the degree to which public policy represents the will of the governed and the extent to which government officials and their decisions are viewed as legitimate by the populace. How would a multiparty system impact on these aspects of American democracy? What other criteria should one consider, and how would change in the political system affect them?

In subsequent chapters we will turn to all of these questions. But the best place to begin exploring this dilemma is with an examination of third parties themselves. We all know that the major parties in the United States are the Democratic and Republican parties. But how many of us know that more than fifty different parties appeared on the ballot in one or more states in the 2000 election? When we think of a "third-party" alternative, do we mean the Libertarian party or the Right-to-Life party or the Socialist Workers party, each of which ran candidates for president and for a number of other offices in recent elections? What are the varieties of "third" parties, which are in fact often fourth, fifth, sixth, or higher-numbered parties in various elections? How do they fit into the dilemma we are exploring?

Varieties and Definitions of Third Parties

When most of us think about third parties in the United States, we think about "third-party" candidates for president. In the most recent elections, that has meant Ross Perot and Ralph Nader. But the 1992 and 1996 Perot campaigns and the 2000 Nader campaign were different on a number of counts, and those differences are important for our consideration.

In 1992 Perot presented himself as an alternative to the candidacies of then–President Bush and his Democratic challenger, Governor Bill Clinton of Arkansas. Perot formed and funded his own organization, **United We Stand America**, and ran an extensive petition drive to win a place on the ballot in all fifty states. He was considered a threat to win the election, or at least to contend seriously for a top spot, and he was included in the major televised debates, essentially as an equal to Bush and Clinton. But there was no third "party" in an organizational sense. Perot the candidate was an alternative to the Republican and Democratic nominees, but United We Stand was not a party in the traditional sense of the word.

Political parties have a formal organizational structure and formal procedures; they contend for a variety of offices; they develop and present platforms that state their views on the issues of the day; they persist for a period of time and win the allegiance of followers because of their candidates, their issue positions, their records of achievement.[1] Ross Perot, a flamboyant Texas billionaire, took advantage of popular dissatisfaction with the political system and the two leading candidates. The organization was the one he bought and paid for, and the procedures were those he chose to follow; he ran alone on a small number of issues that he championed; he came onto the scene quickly and built support because of his charisma and "plain-talkin', roll-up-your sleeves, and get-under-the-hood-and-fix-what's-wrong" style. His organization showed none of the signs of an enduring party.

By 1996, however, some signs pointed to a different situation. In the interim, Perot had financed the formation of the Reform party; as a party it had qualified for the ballot in all fifty states. In order to do so, the Reform party had established at least the semblance of an organization, nationally and in the states; it had established procedures under which its candidates would be chosen. Although the party remained "Perot's party," others challenged his dominance; former Colorado governor Richard Lamm even challenged Perot for the party's presidential nomination. At its national convention and at conventions in a number of states, the party adopted a platform, outlining its stand on a variety of issues. After winning the nomination, Perot agreed to accept federal funding under the provisions of the **Federal Election Campaign Act** (FECA). Other candidates ran on the Reform party label in many states. Thus, the 1996 Perot campaign was a true, emerging third-party campaign in many respects.

Of course, the 1996 campaign was not as successful in terms of votes received and influence as Perot's first effort had been. He never threatened President Clinton in the polls. The bipartisan Commission on Presidential Debates decided that he did not have a legitimate chance to win and excluded him from the televised debates. Perot did not dip endlessly into his own financial reserves and thus spent less than did the two major party candidates in the general election. He spent much of his time trying, unsuccessfully, to convince voters and opinion leaders that he was a serious contender. Although his 8.4 percent in 1996 still ranks him high among the third-party vote totals, it paled in comparison to his 1992 results. Nonetheless, by exceeding 5 percent in 1996, the Reform party was guaranteed funding under the provisions of the FECA for its candidate in 2000, albeit at a reduced level. In 2000, however, the Reform party standard-bearer, Pat Buchanan, polled so few votes that the party lost federal funding for the next presidential election (see Chapter 2).

One of the goals of the Green party in the 2000 election was to exceed the 5 percent threshold needed to be funded in 2004. Throughout the campaign it was clear that Ralph Nader, their candidate, was the most prominent alternative-party choice. However, his poll numbers never reached the level that would have had him included in presidential debates; his vote total fell far short of party expectations. Thus, by the standards applied to the Perot campaigns, Nader's was not a success. If one looks at its impact on the outcome of the presidential race, however, some claim that Nader's effort was more significant than even Perot's in 1992. Because of the extreme closeness of the 2000 presidential contest between George Bush and Al Gore, particularly in a few pivotal states like Florida and New Hampshire, the Nader vote might well have made the difference.

Perot and Nader were not the only "third-party" candidates on the presidential ballot in 1992, 1996, or 2000. In 1996, Harry Browne, the Libertarian party candidate, appeared on all fifty state ballots; he polled nearly 500,000 votes. Ralph Nader, who ran on a number of different labels, all associated with the Green party, appeared on twenty-two state ballots and received write-in votes in fourteen other states. His vote total of nearly 700,000 included almost 250,000 votes in California alone. The Natural Law party candidate, Dr. John Hagelin, and the Taxpayers party standard-bearer, Howard Phillips, appeared on forty-four and thirty-nine state ballots, respectively, though their vote totals were lower than those of Nader or Browne.

In 2000, Browne was again the Libertarian party candidate, appearing on forty-nine state ballots and that of the District of Columbia. Pat Buchanan carried the Reform party banner, also on forty-nine state ballots. Hagelin, as the Natural Law party candidate and under a number of other labels, and Phillips, this time running as the Constitution party candidate, were again running for president, on the ballot in thirty-eight and thirty-one states, respectively. But none of these, or any of the other less "prominent" minor party candidates, polled even 1 percent of the vote, much less than the 5 percent threshold necessary to qualify for federal funds in the next presidential election cycle.

Interestingly, none of these alternative candidates was deemed as important by the media as the potential third-party candidates who did not run in the 1996 election. Early in that election campaign, a group of politicians discontented with their former political parties—King and Lowell Weicker (CT), who had won governorships without major party backing; Lamm, who had yet to announce his challenge to Perot, former U.S. senators and presidential hopefuls Gary Hart (CO) and Paul Tsongas (MA); retiring senator Bill Bradley (NJ); and retired congressman Tim Penny (MN)—toyed with the idea of forming a third political party. Their **trial balloon** was never launched. These men, who came to be known as the Gang of Seven, were experienced and practical enough to know that a new party could not be successful if it did not have a prominent candidate to lead the charge, and none of the luminaries they approached was willing to champion their effort.

Later in 1996, the retired chairman of the Joint Chiefs of Staff, U.S. Army General Colin Powell, was touted as a potential candidate, as either a Republican or an independent. According to a *Time*/CNN poll, respondents rallying behind Powell favored an independent candidacy by about 3:2 over a Republican candidacy (Collet, 1996a); but Powell rejected all overtures and chose to return to the private sector instead. Speculation was rife as to why Powell had refused to run. His professed reason—that he could make a contribution in private life and chose to do so for a time at least—was undoubtedly true, but it also undoubtedly allowed him to avoid mentioning other reasons, including some that dealt with the willingness to undergo the tests and challenges of electoral campaigning, even outside the mantle of the major parties.

It is clear that merely having a choice is not a problem. Minor parties have a long history of running candidates for president. Table 1.1 lists the non-major parties that have held a place on presidential ballots in the last fourteen presidential elections, noting the years in which they ran candidates. What can be learned from this overview of candidates and potential candidates? *First, in most recent elections, if the voters have been looking for a third-party alternative and have not been finding it, what they have really wanted is an alternative viable candidate.*

These non-major party candidates who have run constitute four logical groupings. Consider first those who received the most publicity and the most votes: Henry A. Wallace and J. Strom Thurmond in 1948; George Wallace in 1968; John B. Anderson in 1980; Perot in 1992 and 1996. These were prominent individuals who were dissatisfied with the choices presented in the presidential elections and decided to offer themselves as alternatives. All save Perot had had earlier careers in one or the other of the major parties. George Wallace and John Anderson had contested for their party's nomination in the year they ran for president; Strom Thurmond was the candidate of the states' rights advocates who bolted from the

TABLE 1.1 Non-Major Parties on Presidential Ballots, 1948–2000*

Party	1948	1952	1956	1960	1964	1968	1972	1976	1980	1984	1988	1992	1996	2000	Grand Total
America First							X						X		2
American								X	X			X			3
American							X	X					X		3
American Independent						X		X	X		X				4
American Third Party			X												1
Apathy												X			1
Berely Defense Group						X									1
Big Deal										X					1
Christian Nationalist			X												1
Citizens									X	X					2
Communist						X	X	X	X	X					5
Conservative				X											1
Constitution		2		X	X	X								X	6
Constitutional				X											1
Consumer											X				1
Down With Lawyers									X						1
Economic Recovery												X			1
Freedom and Press						X									1
Grassroots													X		1
Green													X	X	2
Independent								X	X	X	X	X			5
Independent								X	X			X		X	4
Independent Afro-American Unity				X											1
Independent Alliance										X					1

TABLE 1.1 *(continued)*

Party	1948	1952	1956	1960	1964	1968	1972	1976	1980	1984	1988	1992	1996	2000	Grand Total
Independent Grassroots													X		1
Libertarian							X	X		X	X	X	X	X	7
Liberty Union Party													X		1
Looking Back												X			1
Middle Class									X						1
Nation Economic Recovery											X				1
National States' Rights				X	X										2
National Unity Party of Kentucky										X					1
Natural Law												X			1
Natural Law Party												X		X	2
Natural People's League									X						1
New Alliance												X			1
New Alliance											X				1
Peace and Freedom						X			X		X	X			4
Peace and Freedom Party													X		1
People's							X								1
People's Constitution						X									1
People's Party								X							1
Poor Man's		X													1
Populist										X		X			2
Populist											X				1
Progressive	X	X													2
Prohibition	X	X	X	X	X	X		X	X	X	X	X	X	X	13

TABLE 1.1 (continued)

Party	1948	1952	1956	1960	1964	1968	1972	1976	1980	1984	1988	1992	1996	2000	Grand Total
Reform													X	X	2
Restoration								X							1
Right to Life									X						1
Right to Life											X				1
Socialist									X						1
Socialist	X	X						X			X	X			5
Socialist Equality Party													X		1
Socialist Labor	X	2				X	X								5
Socialist Labor				X				X							2
Socialist Workers	X	X	X	2		X	2	X	3	X		X		X	15
Socialist Workers Campaign													X		1
Socialists			X											X	2
States' Rights Democrat	X														1
States' Rights			X												1
Statesman									X						1
Take Back America												X			1
Third												X			1
Third World Assembly											X				1
U.S. Labor								X							1
U.S. Taxpayers Party													X		1
Unaffiliated Independent Party													X		1
United American								X							1

TABLE 1.1 (continued)

Party	1948	1952	1956	1960	1964	1968	1972	1976	1980	1984	1988	1992	1996	2000	Grand Total
United Sovereign Citizens										X					1
Universal						X	X								2
Universal Party					X										1
US Taxpayers												X			1
Vermont Grassroots														X	1
Virginia Conservative				X											1
Workers League											X				1
Workers World											X				1
Workers League										X		X			2
Worker's World									X	X	X	X	X	X	6
Grand Total	**6**	**9**	**6**	**9**	**4**	**1**	**9**	**12**	**13**	**12**	**9**	**16**	**16**	**11**	**162**

Source: Congressional Quarterly's Guide to U.S. Elections (Washington, DC: Congressional Quarterly, Inc., 1994), 3d ed., pp. 457–468. Various *Congressional Quarterly* sources.

*Xs equal one party of that name in the election. Numbers indicate that more than one party used the name to contest the election.

1948 Democratic convention over the civil rights plank in the party platform. In a sense these were all **splinter candidacies**, launched by candidates who tried to split a segment off from one of the major parties. This group can be subdivided as well: Thurmond and Wallace were essentially regional candidates, drawing on dissatisfaction in the South with the Democrats' liberal stands on social issues, whereas the other three were national candidates, appealing for votes throughout the nation to those who shared their sense of dissatisfaction with the policies of the major parties.

The remaining third parties and their candidates can be divided into three groups: short-lived secessionist parties that splintered from one of the majors, traditional **doctrinaire parties**, and **"new" parties** (Inglehart, 1987, 1990; Muller-Rommel, 1990; Muller-Rommel and Pridham, 1991; Collet, 1996b).

The short-lived secessionist third parties in the United States have arisen in times of discontent over the ways in which the major parties were handling dominant issues (Sundquist, 1983). They built an organization throughout a region or the country and ran candidates for many offices; often, the issues were economic and the parties were defined by their ideological place on the political spectrum. The People's (Populist) party that emerged and flourished in the 1890s is a prototypical example of a traditional minor party in the United States. What has been the fate of these parties? In the case of the Republican party in the mid–nineteenth century, that minor party replaced one of the major parties, the Whigs. More frequently, however, either the minor parties' issues have been taken over by one of the major parties or the minor parties have disappeared due to irrelevance.

In addition to these splinter parties, others that arose under similar circumstances assumed a minor position at the fringe of American politics, voicing a concern but winning few supporters; they have become persistent minor parties espousing a clear doctrine. One could say that they, too, were dissatisfied with the major parties and were clear on alternative proposals. But they have been unwilling to make pragmatic compromises and have defined their roles as voicing clear, consistent messages. The Conservative party, the Peace and Freedom party, the Communist party, and the Socialist Workers party exemplify doctrinaire parties in recent years.

The "new" political parties appeal to voters around a different set of issues, issues that reflect differences in cultural more than economic ideologies. Students of comparative politics know that parties of this type are more prominent and more influential in Europe than they are in the United States (Harmel, 1987). The Green party, the Libertarian party, the Natural Law party, and the Right-to-Life party are examples on the contemporary American scene. These parties have had decidedly more success than traditional doctrinaire parties in recent elections. The Nader campaign in 2000 is the prime example of this, demonstrating at the national level (as well as subnational campaigns) that the appeal of these parties can reach enough voters to impact the election, if not necessarily to gain victory. We will return to these minor parties where appropriate throughout this book, but they will not be a major focus of our analysis.

The second lesson learned from recent history is that the nature of modern campaigning means that electoral success for minor party candidates in presidential elections relates more to individual candidate characteristics than to party organization. Perot in 1992 was willing to spend more of his own money than his party could spend in 1996. In 1992, he was new and was viewed as a breath of fresh air; by 1996, he was old hat and began to look just like other politicians. In 1992, it was enough to know what Perot was against; by 1996, people wanted to know what the Reform party was for. Similarly in 2000, voters who viewed environmental concerns as important, as well as some troubled by the corporate nature of American society, were attracted to the Nader campaign, but many others were unsure that the messenger of their discontent would really be an effective leader if in office. For politicians presenting themselves as an alternative to those with whom citizens are dissatisfied, opposition is enough; for parties seeking a permanent role in the American political system, an alternative vision is necessary. The first is easy; the second is more difficult.

Subpresidential Politics

Up to this point, we have discussed third-party politics almost entirely in the context of national—indeed, presidential—politics. What about the role of minor parties in the states? We have pointed out that four recent governors won without major party backing: Ventura in Minnesota, King in Maine, Weicker in Connecticut, and Hickel in Alaska. In most ways, their campaigns have been like the entrepreneurial third-party presidential campaigns discussed above. They have each been prominent individuals in their states. Each left one of the major parties and took off on his own, voicing dissatisfaction with the direction both parties were taking. Although Weicker and Hickel formed political parties to back their campaigns, these were parties in name only. King did not even bother with the pretense of a party. Ventura, by way of contrast, ran on the Reform party label, but in many ways he *became* the Reform party in Minnesota—the embodiment of the party rather than its instrument. None of these men had any significant influence on other statehouse races.

Weicker and Hickel served only one term each, and their parties did not survive them in any real sense. King easily won a second term in Maine, but no third-party movement formed around him. Maine has had a tradition of strong independent, if not third-party, candidates in gubernatorial races; that pattern will continue in 2002 with a well-financed independent candidate who is as independent of King as he is of the two major parties. Ventura remains a popular figure in Minnesota, likely to run for reelection and to be favored in that race, but there is little evidence that his followers are organizing a slate of candidates to support him in office.

A different trend is appearing if one looks at minor party organizations in the states. According to Christian Collet (1997), there has been an explosion of minor parties and candidates running under their labels in recent decades. Whether one looks at those parties that appear on any one year's ballot, or at those that qualify for ballot positions year after year, the number has been rising precipitously.

What has been the impact of these parties? That is difficult to judge, and the answer might well depend on how one defines "impact." Certainly, the rise is indicative of more political activism, especially by those espousing the ideas of the so-called new parties. Whereas once those not in the political mainstream eschewed political involvement, today they are organizing and participating. Increased participation may be viewed as beneficial to the health of a democracy. More individuals are running for office and giving voters who share their views an alternative at the polls.

Yet at the same time, additional candidates on the ballot crowd the field so that voters are often confused as to who stands for what. This crowding does not seem to be a problem in high-salience elections, such as that for president. But when three, four, five, or more candidates enter the race for Congress or the state legislature—and when all candidates are included in every public debate—the waters may indeed be muddied. This confusion is especially evident when one or more of these candidates choose to use attack ads as the primary campaign tactic, which makes it difficult for voters to focus on comparison of the candidates likely to win.

Even if the issues remain clear, the presence and vote-drawing potential of minor party candidates can cloud the election outcome. As an example, in a special election in 1997 to fill the New Mexico congressional seat vacated by Democratic representative Bill Richardson when President Clinton appointed him U.S. ambassador to the United Nations, a minor party enabled the Republicans to win. Richardson's district had long been considered a safe Democratic seat. However, a spirited campaign by the Green party's candidate, who polled 17 percent of the vote, split the Democratic vote so that the Republican candidate gained a winning plurality (43 percent). In the last decade, minor party and independent candidates for Congress have averaged about 2–3 percent of the vote each, and those for governor have averaged nearly 5 percent (Collet, 1997). One such candidate would not necessarily have much of an effect on an election's result, but multiply that by three or four and the "spoiler" role becomes very real.[2] Even if the spoiler role is discounted, vote dilution raises the question of how winners interpret their victory if the vote total is much less than a majority.

The Dilemma of the Two-Party System

This, then, is the dilemma we face. On the one hand, our citizens have expressed a dissatisfaction with the two-party choice presented to them in recent elections. The parties are too much alike. Neither of them is getting the job done. The government is not working for us under the current system.

On the other hand, when presented with alternatives, these same citizens vote for one of the major parties. This result has been the same whether one is considering independent candidacies—which really do not represent third parties but rather entrepreneurial politicians presenting themselves as alternatives—or the minor parties that have contested recent elections.

One could argue that we, the public, are somewhat schizophrenic in that we ask for alternatives but reject them when they are offered. We really are unclear about what we want. But even if a third party—or a number of "third" parties—emerged to contest American elections up and down the ballot, would that be beneficial to the political system? In other words, might we not be better off with the system we have now? Might it not serve our nation and our people better than the untried alternative that some seem to crave (see Lowi, 1996)?

In the chapters that follow, we explore this dilemma. In Chapter 2 we look at the history of third parties in the United States. We examine both the more important third parties and more transient parties, discussing the roles they have played in moving the major parties to different positions on the issues of the day as well as their impact on electoral politics.

In Chapter 3 we explore the constitutional and legal context in which political parties—major and minor—must function. Among the issues discussed are the offices that are contested; the impact of the primary system, the **first-past-the-post** winner system, and the **Electoral College** system; and the influence of the Federal Election Campaign Act and **ballot access** rules on party development. We also look at the roles of state laws, of national legislation, and of the courts in determining the place of minor parties in our system. Understanding the political context in which parties function is critical to understanding why our two-party system has survived.

In Chapter 4 we look at the current level of dissatisfaction with the two major parties and investigate how that dissatisfaction is manifested on the contemporary political scene. We begin to examine the normative considerations regarding the costs and benefits of a two-party system, distinguishing what is happening in states that have experienced non-major party governors from what has occurred in other states and exploring cross-national comparisons.

In Chapter 5 we discuss the likely future of the two-party system in the United States, looking at new parties as well as the Perot phenomenon. We also present our own view on the normative question we have posed: Can the two-party system address the dissatisfaction that is evident within our polity today, or are more fundamental changes—including the presence of viable alternative parties—called for? Finally, we conclude with a discussion of changes that are necessary if the current two-party system is to serve the needs of the polity more satisfactorily.

Throughout these chapters, we focus on our American political system. That is, we are concerned with how independent or third-party candidates serve the needs of those involved in campaigns. We concentrate on whether they have an impact on our nation's politics and governance and on how the citizenry views them. We focus on national politics, but we discuss state politics as well, especially when state experience might be a good predictor of what could happen at the national level were the two-party system altered significantly. We make these choices because they help us to address a puzzling dilemma: Why has our two-party system persisted, and how can we best evaluate it?

2

Minor Parties in a Two-Party System: Historical Perspectives

South Carolina's Democratic governor, J. Strom Thurmond (right) was the Dixiecrat presidential candidate in 1948. His vice presidential running mate was Governor Fielding L. Wright of Mississippi (left).

THE AMERICAN PARTY SYSTEM, which began in the 1790s, has now completed its second century. Since 1854, the same two parties—the Democratic and the Republican—have dominated electoral politics. Both have records of longevity without rival across the globe. Ironically, organized partisanship in the United States was an unplanned development. In their design for the republic, the constitutional framers did not envision a president nominated by party conventions, party-based campaigns and voting, and a Congress organized on the basis of partisanship. Early leaders such as George Washington, James Madison, and Alexander Hamilton believed that parties would be divisive and would undermine the public interest. Fearing the impending rise of political parties, Washington in his 1796 Farewell Address sounded a warning:

> [The spirit of party] serves always to distract the Public Councils and enfeeble the Public administration. It agitates the Community with ill-founded jealousies and false alarms, kindles the animosity of one party against another, foments occasional riot and insurrection. It opens the door to foreign influence and corruption, which find a facilitated access to government itself through the channels of party passions.

Such misgivings about parties have remained a persistent feature of the American political culture. Thus, Progressive reformers in the early twentieth century imposed upon parties state-level regulations, including the requirement that they permit ordinary citizens to participate in selecting party nominees via primary elections, thereby weakening parties in a fundamental way. In the wake of the Watergate scandal of the 1970s, Congress enacted reform legislation restricting party contributions and also aiding the parties' rivals—political action committees (PACs).

In the 1990s, the public's qualms about the Republicans and Democrats were readily recognizable. Public opinion surveys showed consistent majorities preferring to have the presidency and Congress controlled by different parties. In a July 8, 1992, *Washington Post* poll, 82 percent of the respondents agreed with the statement that "both American political parties are pretty much out of touch with the American people." Even more telling was the 18.9 percent of the popular vote garnered by Ross Perot in his independent bid for president in 1992. And in the run-up to the 1996 election, 63 percent of the respondents in another *Post* survey

(November 6, 1995) said they would vote for a third-party candidate for president or Congress.

Public expressions of dissatisfaction with the two major parties and the parties in general continued as the voters contemplated their choices for 2000. A 1998 *Washington Post* poll found that only 8 percent of those questioned believed that party was the most important criterion to use in voting for president, and in December 1999 45 percent expressed dissatisfaction with having to choose between Bush and Gore and wanted a strong third-party alternative ("Many Americans Want Third Party Choice," 1999).

In spite of these polling results reflecting voter dissatisfaction with the Republicans and Democrats, third-party presidential candidates in 1996 and 2000 failed to win a significant share of the voters once they entered the polling booth. After his strong third-place showing in 1992, Perot won only 8.4 percent of the vote as the Reform party candidate in 1996, and with the ultraconservative Pat Buchanan as the party's nominee in 2000, its share of the vote fell to a mere .42 percent. Indeed, the Green party with Ralph Nader as its presidential candidate overtook the Reform party as the third-place finisher.

The inability of Perot, Buchanan, or Nader—despite evidence of voter dissatisfaction—to dent the Republican-Democrat electoral juggernaut demonstrates a fundamental truth about the American party system: It is a system in which two-party dominance has been institutionalized (Epstein, 1986). The United States, however, does not have a pure two-party system. Every year minor parties (fourteen parties ran candidates for president in 2000) appeal to voters. Some, like the Prohibition and Socialist parties, have long histories. But in reality, such doctrinal parties are not operating elements of the party system. Instead, they are like "rivulets alongside the main streams of party life," on the whole maintaining an "isolated existence" (Key, 1964:279). Similarly, the so-called new parties, such as the Green, Natural Law, Libertarian, and Right-to-Life parties, each having a distinctive cultural orientation, also operate largely outside the mainstream party system. These varieties of minor party have had a minimal impact upon American politics and hence are not a focus in this analysis.

Unlike the doctrinal and new parties that operate largely outside the mainstream of American politics, there has been a steady current of "recurring, short-lived, minor party eruptions" that have been intimately connected to the party system (Key, 1964:255). The integral linkage between these parties and the major parties is documented in the survey of American political history that follows in this chapter (see Table 2.1). At various stages in America's development, these minor parties have raised issues not being addressed by the major parties, have affected the outcome of elections, and have helped precipitate major electoral **realignment**. But only one minor party—the Republican party—managed to

TABLE 2.1   Third Parties in American History

Third Party	Year	Percent Popular Votes	Electoral Votes	Fate in Next Election
Anti-Masonic	1832	7.0	7	Endorsed Whig
Free Soil	1848	10.1	0	Received 5% of vote; provided base of Republican supporters
Whig-American	1856	21.5	8	Party dissolved
Southern Democrat	1860	18.1	72	Party dissolved
Constitutional Union	1860	12.6	39	Party dissolved
Populist	1892	8.5	22	Endorsed Democrat
Progressive (T. Roosevelt)	1912	27.5	88	Returned to GOP
Socialist	1912	6.0	0	Received 3.2% of vote
Progressive (La Follette)	1924	16.6	13	Returned to GOP
States' Rights Democrat	1948	2.4	39	Party dissolved and returned to Democrats
Progressive (H. Wallace)	1948	2.4	0	Received 1.4% of vote
American Independent (Geo. Wallace)	1968	13.5	46	Received 1.4% of vote
John B. Anderson	1980	7.1	0	Did not run in 1984
H. Ross Perot	1992	18.9	0	Formed the Reform party; received 8.4% of vote
Reform (Perot)	1996	8.4	0	Received .42% of vote with renegade Republican Pat Buchanan as its nominee
Reform (Buchanan)	2000	.42	0	unknown
Green (Ralph Nader)	2000	2.73	0	unknown

achieve major party status. This was accomplished between 1854 and 1860 while an existing major party—the Whig party—was in the process of dissolution. However, in testimony to the extent to which Democratic-Republican competition has been institutionalized, no party has emerged in almost 150 years to challenge their electoral dominance. Given the obstacles to a new party achieving majority status (described in Chapter 3), it is most unlikely that either the

Republicans or the Democrats will be dislodged as major parties or that the United States will enter an era of multiparty politics.

The Emergence of a Party System

American parties were born in the policy conflicts between the followers of Alexander Hamilton and Thomas Jefferson during Washington's presidency. With the intensification of their disputes, Hamilton and Jefferson turned to supporters in Congress, and factional alliances between leaders in the executive and legislative branches developed. It was the Jeffersonians who first sought to broaden their operations outside the nation's capital by organizing supporters at the state and local levels and endorsing candidates for national and state offices. The Jeffersonians were thus the first real party-builders. Their opponents, dubbed Federalists for their support of a strong national government capable of engaging in nation-building and protecting business interests, were reluctant party organizers. Initially, they bemoaned their rivals' party organizing, as Hamilton acknowledged when he noted that the Federalists "erred in relying so much on the rectitude and utility of their measures as to have neglected the cultivation of popular favor by fair and justifiable expedients" (Key, 1964:203). The Federalists, who belonged to the party of the American elite, paid a heavy price for their failure to respond in as timely a manner as the Jeffersonians had to the popular and democratic style of politics that was developing. They lost the election of 1800 to Jefferson's Democratic-Republicans and went into a precipitous decline thereafter.

During Andrew Jackson's first term in the White House (1829–1833), America's first national third party, the Anti-Masonic party, emerged. It was an early-nineteenth-century version of fundamentalist Christian distrust of the elite establishment and secularism, and it drew most of its support from the poor and revival-minded Protestants. The party focused its wrath upon Free Masonry and its secret rituals, which used the cross and sacred symbols in what the Anti-Masons viewed as a sacrilegious manner. The party lasted only nine years and at its peak controlled twenty-five House seats (1833–1835). The Anti-Masonic party is best remembered for instituting an important democratic innovation: party conventions to nominate presidential candidates and write party platforms (Gillespie, 1993:47–48).

America's first party system was different from any that were to follow because neither those who considered themselves Federalists nor Democratic-Republicans were born into families with these affiliations. As Everett Carll Ladd has noted, "The absence of inherited party loyalties in the new party system . . . together with the rudimentary character of party organization and the prevailing tendency to see party as, at best, a necessary evil, made the new party growth superficial. The roots of party simply did not run deep" (1970:82).

The Pre–Civil War Era: Two-Party Competition, Minor Party Eruptions

Jackson, who won reelection under the Democratic party banner in 1832, followed a course that caused opponents of his policies to coalesce and form an opposition party, the Whig party. In the next two decades, the Democrats and the Whigs engaged in an intense struggle as the dropping of property ownership requirements for voting vastly increased the size of the electorate. The parties engaged in popularized campaigning—torchlight parades, rallies, picnics, campaign songs, and slogans like "Tippecanoe and Tyler, too." In this atmosphere of partisan mobilization, voters began to see themselves as either Whigs or Democrats (McCormick, 1966:342). Unlike the Federalists, who had been reluctant to court popular support, the Whigs sought it with zeal. As the national minority party, the Whig party favored a particular tactic in presidential contests: running military heroes with an appeal beyond the party. Twice, this strategy was successful—in 1840 with William Henry Harrison, and in 1848 with Zachary Taylor.

Both the Whig and the Democratic parties were truly national in that they engaged in relatively close competition in most states (see Figure 2.1). Indeed, between 1836 and 1852, the "United States had less regional variation in voting than at any other time in history" (Ladd, 1970:99). This absence of **sectionalism** reflected the skills of Democratic and Whig leaders in balancing the interests of farmers, manufacturing and mercantile interests, nativists, immigrants, Catholics, and Protestants. The lack of highly salient issues that divided the public along sectional issues contributed to the ability of the two parties to compete successfully on a truly national basis.

Antislavery Parties: Liberty and Free Soil

Periodic minor party eruptions during the Democratic-Whig era were, however, an indication that a major change in the party system was in the offing. Formed in 1840, the Liberty party was the first political party dedicated to the abolition of slavery. Its platform was relatively moderate, calling for elimination of slavery in federally administered areas and prohibiting interstate trade in slaves. With the Whigs and Democrats largely ignoring the issue and newspapers barely mentioning that an abolitionist party had been formed, in addition to lacking an organization base, the Liberty party attracted only 7,000 (.3 percent) voters in 1840. It

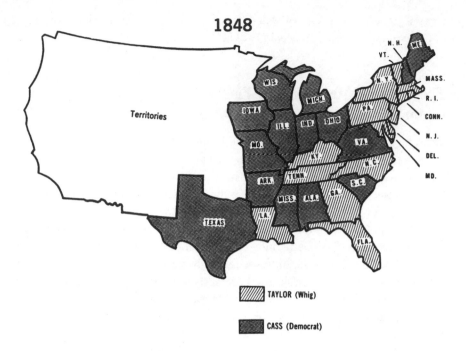

FIGURE 2.1   The 1848 electoral vote map

did little better in 1844 and then split into three factions before disappearing (Rosenstone, Behr, and Lazarus, 1984:49–51).

One of its factions, led by Salmon P. Chase (later a Republican leader and chief justice of the U.S. Supreme Court), formed the Free Soil party in 1848. Chase sought to create a party that was more moderate on abolition than the Liberty party and to gain a broad base of support. The Free Soil party only went so far as to oppose the extension of slavery in newly acquired territories, thereby seeking to win support from Whigs and Democrats in states where slavery already existed. It also advocated cheap postage and, more important, a homestead act to provide land for settlers. As a party emphasizing the needs and interests of free, white labor, its presidential nominee in 1848, former Democratic president Martin Van Buren, gained slightly more than 10 percent of the vote.

As it entered the 1850s, the party built ties to northeastern and midwestern antislavery Democrats. These inroads enabled the Free Soilers to elect two of their leaders, Charles Sumner and Salmon Chase, to the Senate while also electing several members of the House. The Free Soil–antislavery Democratic alliance strengthened antislavery forces in Washington, but it also sapped much of the

Free Soil party's vitality as an independent force. The party then fell under the control of antislavery purists and lost popular appeal. In 1852, its candidate for president received less than 5 percent of the vote. By 1854, the newly formed Republican party had absorbed the Free Soil supporters and organized the antislavery movement into a powerful partisan force that captured the presidency with Abraham Lincoln as its candidate in 1860 (Gillespie, 1993:51–52; Rosenstone, Behr, and Lazarus, 1984:51–56).

A Nativist Party: The American (Know-Nothing) Party

After passage of the Compromise of 1850, which admitted California as a free state and permitted the newly acquired Mexican acquisitions of the New Mexico and Utah Territories to decide the slavery issue by popular sovereignty, another issue gained saliency: immigration policy. The American party was born as an anti-immigrant and anti-Catholic party that appealed to native-born Protestants worried about the huge wave of largely Catholic immigration that began in the 1840s. The party also attracted members through its secret rituals and greetings. Its members' refusal to reveal any information to outsiders led publisher Horace Greeley to dub them the "Know-Nothing party."

In 1854, the Know Nothings had considerable success in gubernatorial and state legislative elections. These quick gains can be attributed to major party decay and the continuing impact of the slavery issue, which was creating divisions among Democrats and giving rise to the Republican party in the North. The Know-Nothings were neutral on the slavery issue and thus attracted voters committed to preserving the Union. In addition, the Know-Nothings benefited from intense anti-immigrant sentiment. However, by 1856 the party was in decline, having failed to implement any of its anti-Catholic and anti-immigrant schemes. But more important, the passage in 1854 of the Kansas-Nebraska Act again made the slavery issue—which had supposedly been resolved by the Compromise of 1850—the nation's primary concern. The Know-Nothing party, built on the basis of nationalism and union, "could no more survive these sectional forces than the union itself" (Billington, 1933:423). Northern Know-Nothings joined the newly formed Republican party, thereby alienating the party's southern supporters. After being taken over by former Whigs, the party in 1856 won 21.5 percent of the vote, mainly in southern states, and then died (Rosenstone, Behr, and Lazarus, 1984:56–59).

The Republicans: A New Major Party

Both the Whigs and the Democrats were unable to reconcile the sectional conflicts within their ranks created by divisions over the slavery issue and the growing economic and cultural differences between the North and the South. While the abolitionist movement gained momentum in the North, demonstrating the force of a compelling moral issue, the South continued to harbor the institution of slavery. In addition, the two regions' economies were developing quite differently. The South continued to concentrate almost exclusively on agriculture, particularly cotton, whereas the North was becoming increasingly industrial, urban, and mixed in its ethnic composition. From its founding in 1854 through 1860, the new antislavery Republican party gathered supporters from disaffected northern Whigs and Democrats and the remnants of the Free Soilers. By 1856, it had emerged as the principal opposition party to the Democrats, when its presidential nominee, John C. Fremont, came in second in the popular vote to Democrat James Buchanan. The deterioration of the old Whig-Democratic party system continued in 1860. In the North, the election was a contest between the nominee of the northern Democrats, Stephen A. Douglas, and the former Whig, Abraham Lincoln, now the Republican candidate; in the South, two transient third parties contested for the presidency. The Southern Democratic party nominated John C. Breckinridge, and a former southern Whig, John Bell, ran as the nominee of the Constitutional Union party.

Neither of these southern-based parties had any long-term future. The Constitutional Unionists were reactionaries who sought to wish away the divisiveness of slavery and thereby save a Union that only armed force could preserve (Gillespie, 1993:57). The Southern Democrats, a breakaway element from the Democratic party, objected to the nomination of Stephen A. Douglas. Their leaders were defenders of slavery who were quite willing to consider withdrawal of the slave states from the Union. With the advent of secession and Civil War, both the Southern Democrats and the Constitutional Unionists ceased to have any reason to exist.

In the four-way presidential election of 1860, no candidate received a majority of the popular vote. Republican Abraham Lincoln received only 39.8 percent of the popular vote but rode to a comfortable Electoral College victory (59.4 percent; see Figure 2.2). With the North's defeat of the Confederacy in the Civil War, a new party system developed in which the dominant Republicans, a northern-based party, contested a Democratic party whose strongest region was the South.

As this brief survey of the pre–Civil War era demonstrates, third parties played a crucial role in creating this new party system by (1) giving salience to the divisive issue of slavery; (2) creating divisions within the Whigs and Democrats and thereby contributing to the decline of the Democrats and the collapse of the Whigs; and (3) developing a new major party—the Republican party.

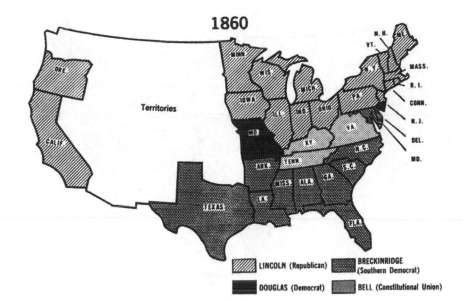

1860

FIGURE 2.2   The 1860 electoral vote map

The Post–Civil War Era: Republican Ascendancy, Sectionalism, Transient Third Parties

The post–Civil War era was a period of Republican dominance. The successful prosecution of the war identified the party with the Union, patriotism, and humanitarianism. But support for the Grand Old Party (GOP) did not rest on emotional issues alone. The Republicans forged a broad electoral alliance with farmers through the Homestead Act and free land in the West, with business and labor through support of a high protective tariff, and with entrepreneurs through federal land grants to build the transcontinental railroad and a permissive noninterference-with-business policy. By imposing Reconstruction on the South, the post–Civil War radical Republicans in Congress forfeited all hope of gaining support among southern white voters, who turned overwhelmingly to the Democrats. Both the Republican and Democratic parties were sectional, with the GOP dominant in the more populous North and the West and the Democrats having overwhelming support in the South (see Figure 2.3).

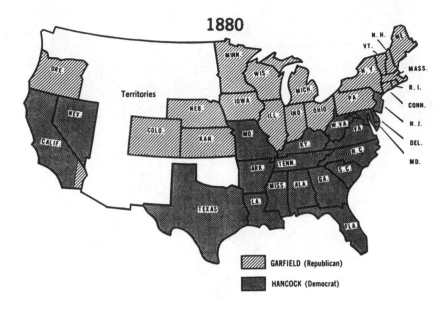

FIGURE 2.3   The 1880 electoral vote map

With the end of Reconstruction in 1876, the two parties started to compete on a more even basis, as the Democrats gained some northern business and farmer allies through their support of free trade while also winning substantial adherents among Roman Catholic immigrants. From the late 1870s until 1896, the Democrats and Republicans alternated control of the presidency and Congress, but the post–Civil War era was primarily an era in which one party dominated the nation's political life.

Schism Among the Republicans: The Liberal Republicans

A faction of the Republican party dissatisfied with the Ulysses S. Grant administration bolted to form its own Liberal Republican party in 1872. Composed of party reformers, anti-Grant politicians, and newspaper editors, this GOP splinter party focused on the corruption of the Grant administration, the need for civil service reform, and ending Reconstruction in the South. Its presidential nominee was Horace Greeley, editor of the *New York Tribune*. In the hope of achieving victory, the Democratic convention endorsed the Liberal Republican candidate and his platform. This cross-party alliance, however, was unsuccessful, as many Democrats refused to vote for Greeley, a longtime Democratic critic.

Underfinanced, organizationally weak, and dependent upon the Democrats for success, the Liberal Republicans went out of business after the 1872 election. Some of the Liberal Republicans' policies were later enacted into law—the curtailment of Reconstruction and the Pendleton Civil Service Act of 1883—but the passage of these measures owed little to the activities of the Liberal Republicans (Gillespie, 1993:62–63).

Parties of Economic Protest: Greenbackers and Populists

Agrarian discontent was rife in the 1870s, spurred by western and southern farmers' discontent with the rates charged by railroads. This discontent resulted in the formation of farmer organizations called "granges," which were dedicated to achieving government regulation of the railroads. The grangers' Anti-Monopoly movement succeeded in 1873 in electing state officials. However, the principal force creating a party of economic protest was the economic panic of 1873, which affected not only farmers but urban workers as well. To solve the nation's economic woes, leaders of the protest movement advocated issuing paper currency—greenbacks—to provide needed capital to hard-pressed farmers, workers, and industries. The National Independent party (commonly known as the Greenback party) was the first to achieve national prominence by coalescing agrarian and labor interests as it merged farmer organizations with small state and local labor reform groups (Gillespie, 1993:65). The high point of its strength was in the midterm elections of 1878, when it won fourteen House seats and collected more than 1 million votes. However, returning economic prosperity, splits among its labor and agrarian leadership, and the prospect of fusion with one of the major parties all undermined the Greenback party. Its presidential candidate in 1884 received only 1.7 percent of the vote.

With the demise of the Greenbackers, most of the party's supporters moved into the People's (Populist) party, an agrarian reform movement that swept across the West and South in the 1890s. Deteriorating conditions on midwestern and southern farms caused by overproduction and world competition politicized farmers, who blamed their plight upon such visible causes as high railroad rates and a shrinking currency supply. Their platform for the 1892 election was far-reaching and radical. In addition to calling for government ownership of railroads and free coinage of silver, it also advocated a graduated income tax, direct election of senators, and reducing the workday to eight hours. In the 1892 election, the Populist presidential candidate, James B. Weaver (the former Greenback candidate of 1880), polled more than 1 million votes (8.5 percent) and carried five states in the Midwest and West. Two years later, its candidates gained 1.5 million votes and elected six senators and seven members of the House.

The emergence of the Greenbackers and Populists as well as the rise of labor organizations reflected the economic dislocations that were being created by the new industrial-urban order that was transforming the nation. Neither the Republican nor the Democratic party was initially responsive to these popular protest movements. However, in 1896 the forces of agrarian radicalism captured the Democratic nomination for William Jennings Bryan, a free-silver Democrat, whose platform was a challenge to the developing industrial order. The key plank in the Democrats' platform was a call for free and unlimited coinage of silver and gold at a ratio of 16:1. In adopting this position, the Democrats appropriated the principal program of the Populists and made a dramatic appeal to farmers, debtors, and western mining interests. The party also advocated low tariffs.

The Populists were now faced with the dilemma of either endorsing Bryan and losing their party's identity or running their own candidate and thereby splitting the free-silver vote. They chose fusion with the Democrats and endorsed Bryan. After that, most Populists remained in the Democratic party, and although the Populist party continued to run candidates until 1908, it never again gained more than 0.8 percent of the vote. The Populists were never able to expand their base beyond the agrarian reform movement, although during the Progressive Era of the twentieth century several of their reform proposals, such as establishing the income tax and direct election of senators, were successful.

The 1896 Election: Electoral Realignment, Republican Resurgence

In the face of the Democrats having embraced populism through the nomination of Bryan, the Republicans in 1896 sought to bolster their post–Civil War coalition by advocating the gold standard and by opposing inflationary free coinage of silver; and they reasserted their position as the defenders of the high protective tariff. Although their stand on the silver issue cost them support in western states, advocacy of a high protective tariff brought the Republicans renewed support among urban workers, who blamed the depression of the 1890s on the low tariff policies of the Democratic Grover Cleveland administration. William McKinley, the GOP nominee, ran on the themes of "Prosperity—Sound Money—Good Markets—Employment for Labor—A Full Dinner Bucket." The Republican cause was significantly aided by the overwhelming support provided by business interests—led by Ohio industrialist Mark Hanna—that were terrified of Bryan and his policies.

The election of 1896 transformed the political landscape as the electorate was realigned and the Republicans gained an infusion of support, especially among urban workers in the Northeast. Bryan's appeal was sectional—in the South, the Plains states, and silver-mining states of the West. He had little appeal for the industrializing East and Midwest, where the bulk of the population and electoral votes were concentrated (see Figure 2.4). In assessing the election of 1896, V. O. Key Jr., the leading scholar of American parties, observed that the Democratic loss "was so demoralizing and so thorough that the party made little headway in regrouping its forces until 1916" (1955·11). Indeed, the Democrats were able to elect only one president between 1896 and 1928—and Woodrow Wilson's election in 1912 was made possible only because of a major split among the dominant Republicans.

Progressivism and the Emergence of the New Deal Democratic Coalition

Although the Republicans gained renewed strength through the electoral realignments that occurred in the wake of the 1896 election, there were serious internal divisions within the party between the Stalwarts (traditional conservatives and their allies in the industrial-financial centers of the Northeast) and the Progressive reformers of the Midwest and West. In 1912 and again in 1924, these festering rifts broke wide open as reformist Republican leaders split the party and sought the presidency under the Progressive banner.

Theodore Roosevelt, after failing in 1912 to wrest the GOP nomination from his handpicked successor, President William Howard Taft, ran as the candidate of the Progressive (Bull Moose) party. Roosevelt was able to outpoll the regular Republican ticket, headed by Taft, but in the process split the GOP vote and enabled Democrat Woodrow Wilson to win the presidency with 41.8 percent of the vote.

Although Roosevelt's splinter candidacy had a major impact on the electoral fortunes of the Democrats as well as the Republicans, his experiment with third-partyism was as brief as it was dramatic. He returned to the Republican fold in 1916 and endorsed its nominee, New York governor Charles Evans Hughes.

In addition to the Bull Moose phenomenon, the 1912 election is also noteworthy because the Socialist party, led by Eugene V. Debs, achieved 6 percent—its all-time highest share of the popular vote. Its relative success early in the twentieth century reflected its ability to appeal to the economically disadvantaged farmers, miners, and lumberjacks through its populist ideas and to immigrants with socialist allegiances in their native countries. The party, however, fell into disarray during World War I due to its opposition to Wilson's preparedness program and its call for a referendum on entering the war. These antiwar proposals damaged the party's image and resulted in attempts at suppression by government officials.

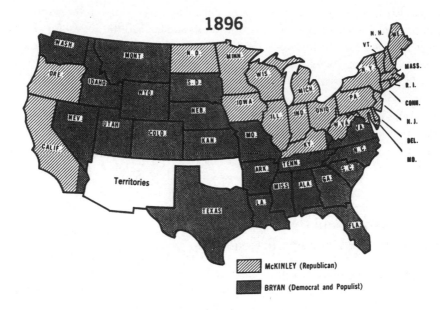

FIGURE 2.4   The 1896 electoral vote map

By the 1920s, the Socialist party had ceased to be an alliance of farmers, unionists, and immigrants. Instead, it was taken over by intellectuals and lost most of its public support (Rosenstone, Behr, and Lazarus, 1984:88–91).

Like Roosevelt's Bull Moose party, the Progressive party that emerged in the 1920s was a Republican reform movement, this time led by Senator Robert La Follette of Wisconsin. But unlike the middle- and upper-class Roosevelt-led party, La Follette's Progressive party of 1924 was based primarily upon farmer and labor support. La Follette's platform denounced corporate monopolies and gave special emphasis to the plight of farmers while also calling for nationalization of rail-roads, development of the federal electric power plant at Muscle Shoals (a fore-runner of the Tennessee Valley Authority), protection of collective bargaining, di-rect primaries, approval of wars by referendum, election of federal judges, and an end to the use of injunctions to stop labor disputes (Rosenstone, Behr, and Lazarus, 1984:95–96; Gillespie, 1993:89). La Follette won 16.6 percent of the pop-ular vote (4.8 million), mainly in agrarian regions west of the Mississippi River, but carried only his home state of Wisconsin.

His campaign suffered from the same problems that plague most independent candidacies: difficulty getting on the ballot in states, lack of financing, inadequate organization, and an absence of candidates running under the Progressive label for congressional and state offices. After La Follette's weak showing, the party was undermined by rising commodity prices for farmers as well as labor unionists' lack of interest in a third party. Because the Progressive party had largely been composed of La Follette's personal following, his death in 1925 caused it to collapse as a national force. However, his sons went on to lead a state-level Progressive party in Wisconsin between 1934 and 1946 (Rosenstone, Behr, and Lazarus, 1984:93–97).

The Ascendancy of the New Deal Democratic Coalition

The La Follette candidacy reflected conflicts and dislocations within American society that were not being addressed by either the Republicans or Democrats. These concerns took on heightened urgency with the stock market crash of 1929 and the Great Depression of the 1930s. The 1932 election of Democrat Franklin D. Roosevelt was a benchmark in American political history. It marked an electoral realignment that ended Republican dominance, as well as the creation of a Democratic electoral majority. Like the Republican coalition that had preceded it, Roosevelt's **New Deal Democratic coalition** was an amalgam of disparate and sometimes conflicting elements. White Southerners, still wedded to white supremacy, were a core group, as were Catholics, blue-collar workers, Jews, and blacks. In addition, young voters entering the ranks of the electorate in the 1930s and 1940s became Democrats. The Democrats were riding a wave of demographic change as urban ethnics, Catholics, blue-collar workers, and blacks were becoming a larger proportion of the electorate, whereas the traditional Republican base of white Protestants, small-town residents, farmers, and middle-class businessmen constituted a declining share of the population.

The New Deal Democratic electoral coalition forged by Franklin Roosevelt proved to be an enduring alliance. From 1932 through 1948, the Democrats controlled the White House and only lost control of the Congress once, in 1946. However, the conflicts inherent in the coalition began to create unity problems by the late 1930s as conservative southern Democrats dissented from Roosevelt's social welfare policies.

Signs of Strain in the Democratic Coalition: The Dixiecrats of 1948

The North-South split in the party became more pronounced in 1948 as segregationist Southerners already unhappy about President Harry Truman's civil rights

program bolted their party's convention when northern Democrats, led by Minneapolis mayor Hubert Humphrey, insisted on a strong civil rights plank in the
platform. The so-called Dixiecrats formed the States' Rights party and nominated
Governor J. Strom Thurmond of South Carolina as their presidential candidate.
The Dixiecrats did not run candidates for offices other than president and vice
president and did not attempt to form an independent party organization. Instead, they sought to use the existing Democratic organizations within their states
and even succeeded in several instances in placing Thurmond's name on the ballot as the official Democratic nominee. He carried four Deep South states in the
election while winning only 2.4 percent of the popular vote and failing to achieve
the movement's basic objective: preventing Truman's reelection (see Figure 2.5).

The Dixiecrat party ceased to exist after the 1948 election as most of its members returned to the Democratic party. Even Thurmond described the whole
episode as a mere "fight within our family." The Dixiecrat movement was, however, a sign that the long-standing alliance between the party's northern and
southern wings was in a fragile state and that major electoral changes were not far
off. Indeed, only four years later, Dwight Eisenhower made major inroads into all
elements of the New Deal Democratic coalition and notably carried four states of
the old Confederacy—Florida, Tennessee, Texas, and Virginia.

The process of disintegrating Democratic support among white Southerners
continued in 1964. With conservatives having captured the Republican nomination for Senator Barry Goldwater (AZ), the GOP won the electoral votes of five
Deep South states, even though President Lyndon Johnson, himself a Texan,
swept to a Democratic national landslide. That same year, Thurmond became one
of the first prominent Southerners to leave the Democratic party and become a
Republican. Viewed from the perspective of the early twenty-first century, the
Dixiecrat revolt can be seen as the beginning of the realignment of southern
white voters away from their traditional Democratic moorings.

Henry Wallace: Rumbling on the Democrats' Left

Henry A. Wallace had served as Roosevelt's secretary of agriculture and was his
third-term vice president. However, under pressure from southern conservatives,
Roosevelt allowed Wallace to be dropped from the ticket in 1944, but Wallace
was retained in the cabinet as secretary of commerce. With the end of World War
II and the Cold War heating up, Wallace became a vocal critic of the Truman administration's foreign policy. Wallace believed in a strong United Nations and
sensitivity to Soviet fears. In becoming the presidential candidate of the Progressive party of 1948, Wallace had hoped for support from organized labor and

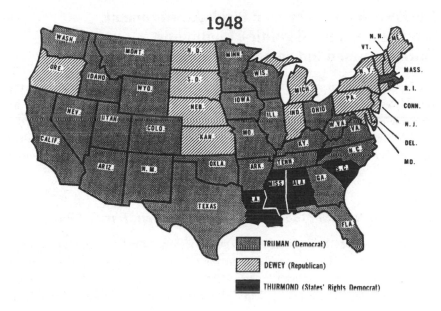

FIGURE 2.5   The 1948 electoral vote map

other liberal interests. Truman, however, undercut Wallace's efforts to secure the unions' support by vetoing the Taft-Hartley Act, a labor relations law bitterly opposed by organized labor. The president's campaign rhetoric also became more liberal as he advocated national health insurance, increases in the minimum wage, federal aid to education, and civil rights legislation. With the liberal press saying that Wallace's campaign could lead to a Republican victory, Wallace's only organized base of support came from the extreme left of American politics—the Communist party and the American Labor party.

Wallace had no real hope of winning the election. He was seeking through his candidacy to show strong opposition to Truman's policies. In this he failed, receiving only 2.4 percent of the vote, half of which came from New York. Wallace's third party was the first to be launched because of foreign policy. But advocating a soft line toward the Soviet Union at a time when Communists were perceived as a threat to national security and the economy was in good shape caused Wallace's protest movement to fizzle, and his version of the Progressive party disappeared (Rosenstone, Behr, and Lazarus, 1984:103–107). Interestingly, however, foreign policy issues were later to become highly salient and cause more severe divisiveness for Democrats in the late 1960s and 1970s as a result of controversies surrounding U.S. involvement in the Vietnam War.

The Post–New Deal System: Divided Government, Candidate-Centered Politics, Continuing Third-Party and Independent Candidacies

The New Deal era of American politics effectively came to an end in 1968 as the Republicans captured the presidency with Richard Nixon as their nominee. By 1968, the Democrats were badly divided by issues of race, the Vietnam War, defense policy, crime and civil disorder, and social policy. Nixon effectively exploited these divisions, winning a narrow popular vote victory over Democrat Hubert Humphrey.

George Wallace and the American Independent Party, 1968

The turmoil within the Democratic party was reflected by the presence of a right-wing splinter candidate for president in 1968, Democrat George Wallace, governor of Alabama. His American Independent party sought to capitalize on the bitter reactions, particularly among white blue-collar workers opposed to civil rights activism, urban riots, anti–Vietnam War demonstrations, and heavy federal spending for President Johnson's Great Society social programs. Wallace carried five southern states and won 13.5 percent of the vote as he drew support from many traditional Democratic voters and thereby reduced Nixon's vote among disaffected Democrats (see Figure 2.6).

Wallace returned to the Democratic party after 1968 and sought the party's presidential nomination in 1972, but a failed assassination attempt left him severely wounded and partially paralyzed. The American Independent party, which he founded, floundered without him as its leader and collapsed after the 1976 election. Wallace, however, had a profound effect on American politics. His presence in the 1968 campaign and his continuing influence caused Nixon to adopt a campaign strategy and governmental policies designed to avoid alienating southern white voters (Rosenstone, Behr, and Lazarus, 1984:113–114). For Democrats, Wallace was an ever-present symbol of their North-South divide and declining support among white Southerners.

Although Nixon won a landslide reelection in 1972, his party was unable to gain control of the Congress, which remained firmly in Democratic hands. This pattern of divided party control of the government, which had been in place during the last six years of the Eisenhower presidency, was thus reestablished during the Nixon years. Indeed, divided government became the norm after 1968 under Republican presidents Nixon, Gerald Ford, Reagan, and George Bush. With the Republican sweep in the midterm elections of 1994, a Democratic president, Bill

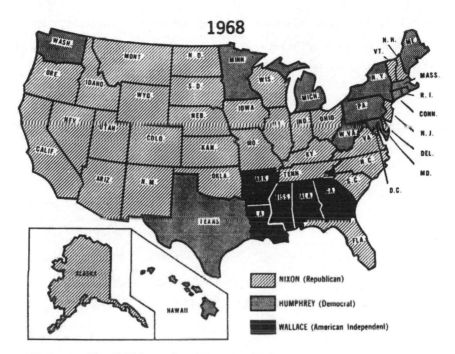

FIGURE 2.6   The 1968 electoral vote map

Clinton, was also forced to coexist with a Congress controlled by the opposition party. And just a few months into his presidency, Republican George W. Bush was forced to contend with opposition party control of the Senate after newly re-elected Senator James Jeffords of Vermont bolted the GOP to become an indepen-dent, thereby handing the Democrats a narrow chamber majority (see Table 2.2).

The commonplace nature of divided party control of the government reflected fundamental changes that were occurring in American politics in the post-1964 era. Among the most significant of these changes were the following:

1. Changes in partisanship, most notably among black voters, who became overwhelmingly Democratic as their numbers swelled due to the civil rights movement and voting rights legislation, and among southern whites, who shifted to the GOP.
2. A weakening of partisan ties among voters generally, as a declining per-centage of citizens came to view even one party favorably.
3. Candidate-centered campaigns with voter choices becoming less influ-enced by partisanship.

TABLE 2.2   Divided Partisan Control of the Presidency and Congress, 1953–2002

Single-Party Control of Government	*Divided-Party Control of Government*
Republican President, House, and Senate 1953–1955 (Eisenhower)	*Republican President, Democratic House and Senate* 1955–1961 (Eisenhower) 1969–1977 (Nixon, Ford) 1987–1993 (Reagan, Bush)
Democratic President, House, and Senate 1961–1969 (Kennedy, Johnson) 1977–1981 (Carter) 1993–1995 (Clinton)	*Republican President, Democratic House, Republican Senate* 1981–1987 (Reagan) *Democratic President, Republican House and Senate* 1995–2001 (Clinton)
	Republican President and House, Democratic Senate 2001–2002 (George W. Bush)
Total of 16 years of single-party control	Total of 34 years of divided control

4. Heightened split-ticket voting, as voters cast ballots for different parties for presidential, congressional, and state offices. (Aldrich and Niemi, 1996)

The electorate's declining partisanship and its less than positive attitude toward either of the major parties provided a hospitable environment for significant independent candidacies for president in 1980, 1992, 1996, and 2000.

The Independent Candidacy of John B. Anderson, 1980

In 1960, Republican John B. Anderson was elected to Congress as a conservative from Rockford, Illinois, but over the course of his House career he moved gradually to the center. This shift caused him to become the target of right-wing activists, who mounted a fierce challenge to his renomination in 1978. Anderson won the congressional primary, but knowing he would again be targeted by the extreme right, he elected to run for president and speak out against those who believed he should find a political home outside the GOP (Broder, 1980:207; Rosenstone, Behr, and Lazarus, 1984:117).

Anderson's campaign in the Republican presidential primaries made little headway against the more prominent candidates, Ronald Reagan and George Bush. He did, however, attract considerable and favorable press attention. After abandoning his quest for the GOP nomination, Anderson became an independent candidate for president. His candidacy was boosted by the perceived weaknesses of the major party candidates. Jimmy Carter had developed the image of a weak and indecisive president, and Ronald Reagan was thought by many to be an aging conservative warhorse with views that were too far right. Anderson had hoped to be the centrist choice between the major party candidates. His financial and organizational back-ing, however, came primarily from individuals on the liberal side of the political spectrum. As a result, he was viewed primarily as a threat to Carter's reelection and was subjected to attacks by Carter that portrayed him as a creation of the media and just another Republican (Rosenstone, Behr, and Lazarus, 1984:118). Not want-ing to give legitimacy and publicity to Anderson's candidacy, Carter even refused to participate in a presidential debate in which Anderson was invited to take part. Lacking an emotional issue, underfinanced, and without an organization base, An-derson received 6.6 percent of the vote, and in the view of political analysts he was not a determining factor in Carter's defeat. He ran most strongly among young and well-educated voters. His support was marginally higher among Democrats than Republicans. The fact that a candidate such as Anderson could do as well as he did was probably attributable to substantial public discontent with the major party candidates (Rosenstone, Behr, and Lazarus, 1984:119).

Continuing Dissatisfaction with Major Party Candidates: Ross Perot, 1992 and 1996

With the public in an angry mood and blaming the Republican administration of George Bush for the state of the economy, an unusually united Democratic party in 1992 nominated Bill Clinton, governor of Arkansas. Clinton was a vulnerable candidate because of allegations about his personal life. Into this seemingly weak field of candidates stepped the folksy and flamboyant Texas billionaire H. Ross Perot, who used CNN's *Larry King Live* to announce his candidacy as an indepen-dent in 1992. With a "can-do" style and a call to throw the rascals out by "cleaning out the barn," Perot had a populist outsider appeal. With ample personal financ-ing, he used infomercials, replete with economic charts and graphs, to dramatize his contention that the country was in "deep voodoo" (an ingenious synthesis of two well-known Bush sound bites; Gillespie, 1993:131). Perot also effectively ex-ploited TV interview programs and paid spot ads; by June 1992 a Harris poll re-ported him leading both Bush and Clinton.

However, early summer 1992 was the high point of Perot's popularity. His cam-paign suffered from his tendency to make unfortunate offhand comments, an inexperienced campaign staff, and his temporary withdrawal from the campaign during the Democratic convention. However, Perot did effectively dramatize and give salience to the issue of ballooning federal deficits and the goal of a balanced budget.

Perot's showing at the polls—18.9 percent of the popular vote—was the strongest of any third-party or independent candidate since Theodore Roosevelt's in 1912. He did not, however, have sufficiently concentrated support to win a single state's electoral votes.[1] Nonetheless, it was a remarkable showing for a political novice, albeit an unusually well financed novice. The 1992 election reflected public dissatisfaction with the two major parties and their candidates. But it also demonstrated the continuing strength and institutionalized nature of the two-party system. Thus, 21 percent of voters who rated Perot as their first choice for president did not vote for him out of fear they were wasting their votes (Abramson et al., 1995:360).

Perot kept his political operation alive after 1992 through fifty state chapters of his public policy organization, United We Stand America. He also sought to maintain his visibility by engaging in a nationally televised debate with Vice President Al Gore, in which he attacked the North American Free Trade Agreement. Again using Larry King's TV program, he announced in 1995 that he was creating a new political party, which he named the Reform party.

Although professing that he did not want to run again in 1996, he easily secured the new party's nomination, despite a challenge by former Colorado governor Richard Lamm. Unlike in 1992, Perot did not engage in lavish personal financing of his campaign. Instead, he agreed to accept $29 million in federal funding, which he was entitled to based upon his showing in the 1992 election. His campaign was similar to that of 1992 in that it relied heavily on TV interview programs, spot ads, and infomercials. For the public, however, the glow was off his candidacy. Polls showed his support during the summer and early fall at only 4–7 percent and also revealed that voters used such terms as "rich," "egotistical," and even "crazy" to describe him. In a severe blow to his campaign's credibility, the Commission on Presidential Debates decided not to include him in the debates on the grounds that he had no "realistic chance" of being elected.

Perot got a small boost late in the campaign by emphasizing the theme of governmental corruption following reports of improper foreign contributions to the Democrats. In the end, he received 8.4 percent of the vote—a dramatic falloff from his nearly 19 percent total in 1992. However, 8 percent was sufficient to ensure that his Reform party was eligible for $12.6 million in federal funding in 2000. In addition, his party would qualify for the ballot in nearly every state. Perot thus became the first independent candidate to gain double-digit popular support, to come back to run four years later, and to launch a new national party. The 1996 election, however, revealed fundamental weaknesses within the Reform party. It was to a large extent a personal vehicle for Perot and was unable to take the necessary steps to become a real party that runs candidates for congressional, state, and local offices, operates open nominating processes, and prepares itself to govern.

Elections 2000: Reform Party Disintegration and Green Party Emergence

The Reform Party Self-Destructs

Although its 1996 election showing assured the Reform party of ballot access in all the states and $12.6 million in federal funds for the 2000 presidential election, such advantages were not enough to save the party from the ravages of chaotic internal divisiveness and an ineffective candidate. After failing to do well in the Iowa straw poll in 1999, television commentator and candidate for the Republican nomination in 1992 and 1996, Pat Buchanan, dropped out of the race for the Republican nomination. Instead he focused his energies on securing the Reform party nomination after associates of Ross Perot invited him to do so. Buchanan shared some of the traditional Reform party issue positions, especially its opposition to free trade, but he stressed conservative social policy positions—opposition to abortion, gay rights, and affirmative action—that divided the party's supporters. He won the Reform party nomination in a contest between himself and John Hagelin, a physicist and advocate of transcendental meditation who had previously run on the Natural Law ticket. The Reform convention, however, was so divisive that it degenerated into two separate conventions—one nominating Buchanan, the other Hagelin—with both candidates claiming to be the true Reform party nominee and therefore entitled to the party's public funding. The Federal Election Commission later ruled in favor of Buchanan. Buchanan's nomination caused Jesse Ventura, the Minnesota governor and the only Reform party candidate to be elected to major statewide office, to quit the party; Ross Perot ended up endorsing George W. Bush.

With the Reform party wracked by internal feuding and Buchanan being kept off the campaign trail due to gallbladder surgery, the Reform party's share of the popular vote for president fell to only .42 percent. Its strongest showings were in North Dakota (3 percent) and Alaska and Idaho (2 percent). Exit polls revealed that only 1 percent of those who had voted for Perot in 1996 voted for Buchanan in 2000. After 2000, then, the party was a mere shadow of its former self—lacking leadership, any semblance of internal unity, and the prospect of federal funding in 2004.

Did the Buchanan Candidacy Affect the 2000 Outcome?

In close elections, as in 2000, the potential for minor parties to influence the outcome is always present. One of the intriguing questions left over from that election is whether Buchanan's candidacy affected the final result. Most of the attention was focused upon Florida and how Nader's almost 100,000 votes siphoned support from Al Gore, thereby costing him twenty-five critical electoral votes. There were, however, four states (Iowa, New Mexico, Oregon, and Wisconsin) with thirty-one electoral votes collectively that went for Gore by margins of less than .5 percent; it is possible, though not probable or likely, that Bush could have won pluralities had Buchanan not been on the ballot (Burden, 2001:12). Had these states gone for Bush, Florida and its Nader vote would not have taken on the importance that they did.

Post-2000 Reform Party Adopts a
Hard-Edged Right-Wing Stance

With less than one-third of its 600 authorized delegates in attendance and only thirty-seven states represented, many with only one delegate, the Reform party's 2001 convention was held in Nashville. Sparsely attended by diehard remnants of the party, it adopted a hard-edged conservative platform that called for tough new anti-immigration legislation, opposition to amnesty for illegal immigrants, severing international trade alliances, repeal of the *Roe v. Wade* decision that legitimized abortion, opposition to fetal-tissue research, defining marriage as between a man and a woman, opposition to hate-crimes laws, restoring God in the public square, and returning the nation to its Christian roots. In remaking itself in the image of Pat Buchanan and his ideology, it seems unlikely that the Reform party will regain the following and influence it carried in 1992 and 1996.

Perot's Legacy: Perot Voters and the Republican
Victories in the 1994 and 2000 Elections

Perot's 18 percent of the vote in 1992 created a powerful incentive for both of the major parties to make a run at the Perot supporters. Under the leadership of conservative GOP House leader Newt Gingrich, the Republicans crafted a campaign manifesto—the Contract with America—that made a focused appeal for the Perot vote. As political scientists Walter Stone and Ronald Rapoport have demonstrated, two-thirds of these voters shifted to the Republicans in the 1994 midterm elections. In House districts where Perot had run strongly in 1992, Perot voters from 1992 accounted for almost half of the net pickup for Republican congressional candidates in 1994. Thus, one of the legacies of the Perot candidacy was a contribution to the Republican takeover of the House in 1994 (Stone and Rapoport, 2001:53).

The Perot candidacy had no real impact on the presidential contest of 1996, which President Clinton won easily. Only one in three of Perot's 1992 supporters continued to support him; 44 percent backed Republican Bob Dole, 22 percent Clinton. However, former Perot voters did have an impact in 2000. Among 1996 Perot voters, approximately 64 percent voted for Bush, only 27 percent for Gore. Stone and Rapoport estimated that Bush achieved a net gain from the collapse of the Reform party of 3 percent of the popular vote (2001:53). In the critical state of Florida, where Perot had gained 9 percent of the vote in 1996, Bush's advantage over Gore among these former Perot voters was almost three to one.

The research of Stone and Rapoport shows that Perot's third-party movement had a significant impact on the party system, given the close relationship between the vote for Perot and the likelihood of voting Republican in ensuing elections. The Perot phenomenon highlights the fact that three conditions need to be present for a third party to have a lasting effect on the party system: (1) It must have a large and identifiable constituency; (2) following the election in which the third party appears, one or both of the major parties must make a bid for the third party's supporters on the basis of issues that motivated them; and (3) the third party's supporters have to respond to a major party's bid and shift their support (Stone and Rapoport, 2001:51).

Ralph Nader and the Green Party: Challenging the Democrats

Although the Buchanan candidacy was a potential threat from the right to the Republicans in 2000, the collapse of the Reform party led by Buchanan did not play a spoiler role in the election and prevent George W. Bush from being elected. The Democrats, however, were not so fortunate thanks to the threat from the left posed by consumer-anticorporate-environmental activist Ralph Nader's candidacy on the Green ticket. Nader had been the Green party nominee in 1996 but had not campaigned actively. However, in 2000 he ran a vigorous campaign on anti–free trade and environmental themes and gained substantial media coverage. Nader charged that Gore was at best the "lesser of two evils" and refused to throw his support to Gore despite pressure from liberal Democrats such as Jesse Jackson and Minnesota senator Paul Wellstone.

Nader ran much stronger than Buchanan, picking up 2.7 percent of the national vote garnering 10 percent in Alaska, 7 percent in Vermont, and 6 percent in Hawaii, Maine, Massachusetts, Montana, and Rhode Island. Most of Nader's votes came at the expense of Gore. This was especially important in closely contested states. Most analysts believe that had Nader not been on the ballot, Gore would have carried Florida and other states won narrowly by Bush (e.g., New Hampshire and Tennessee) and won the Electoral College majority. Exit polls conducted by Voter News Service showed that in a two-candidate race between Bush and Gore 47 percent of the Nader voters would have picked Gore, 21 percent Bush; 32 percent would not have voted. In spite of its impact on the 2000 race, the Green party led by Nader failed to achieve the 5 percent of the vote needed to qualify for federal funding in 2004; this would have allowed the party to pursue its environmental and anti–free trade agenda more effectively.

The Nader vote came mainly from those who supported Clinton or abstained in the 1996 election, with a modest contribution from former Perot voters. Nader tended to win votes from white, liberal, yet nonpartisan voters discontented with the economy. As with other minor party movements that have often owed their support to anti-incumbent sentiment, Nader voters tended to hold Gore responsible for an imperfect economy. As Harvard political scientist Barry Burden has observed, "Nader occupied a niche that attracted those with higher educations and lower incomes" (2001:14). He also gained support among younger voters.

One of the most unusual aspects of the Nader candidacy is that his standing in the polls actually rose during the final weeks of the campaign. Normally, third-party support fades as Election Day draws closer. This pattern has held since the 1924 campaign of Robert La Follette through John Anderson in 1980 and Ross Perot's 1992 run for the presidency. The only exception (until Nader in 2000) was J. Strom Thurmond's regionally concentrated southern support in 1948 (Rosenstone, Behr, and Lazarus, 1996:41).

Turnout Effects of Nader and Buchanan in 2000

It has been estimated that the Nader and Buchanan candidacies increased overall voter turnout by 2.5 percent by causing persons to go to the polls who might otherwise have abstained from voting in a two-way race between Bush and Gore. Burden has noted that many of Nader's supporters "were so committed to him— or dissatisfied with every other candidate—that they simply would have abstained had Nader not run. It is this relationship between voters' enthusiasm and their candidates' votes share that allows some of the poorest performing minor parties to have some of the largest direct effect on voter turnout" (2001:9).

Minor Parties in State Politics

State-level political alignments of voters have tended to follow the national—particularly the presidential—alignment of voters. Thus, throughout the long period of Republican-Democratic party dominance since the 1850s, partisan electoral competition for state offices has been mainly between the Republicans and Democrats, just as it has been for Congress and the presidency. Even during the second party system, that of the Democrats and Whigs, national-party labels were used in state elections. As V. O. Key Jr. has observed, "The government system may be federal, but the voter in the polling booth usually is not" (1956:33).

Even though state and local party organizations have frequently been more concerned about winning state and local offices than national offices, these organizations and their candidates have made effective use of their national parties' followings for their own constituencies.

With the same two-party electoral alignment of Republicans versus Democrats at the national and state levels, the American party system stands in sharp contrast to Canada's. Our neighbor to the north has had persistent regionally based third parties capable of winning power in provincial governments and the national legislature (Epstein, 1986:124). Thus, in the 1997 national elections, regionally based parties succeeded in capturing 41.5 percent of the seats in the Canadian House of Commons: The right-wing Reform party won a majority of seats from the western provinces of Alberta, British Columbia, and Saskatchewan; the Bloc Quebeçois carried Quebec; and the New Democrats were dominant in the Yukon Territory. The western-based Reform party constituted the largest opposition party in the House of Commons, in which the Liberal party, a major party, held a majority. A similar pattern continued in the 2000 Canadian elections. Regionally based parties again won more than 40 percent of the vote, and only the victorious Liberal party, with its stronghold in the province of Ontario, could claim to have won at least one House of Commons seat in each province.

The pragmatic and flexible character of American parties has enabled them to accommodate considerable variety among state and local affiliates and to absorb and discourage most deviant groups. With their control of national patronage through appointments of federal judges, U.S. attorneys, and regional administrators of selected federal programs, the major parties impose a special obstacle for independent, state-based minor parties. And when third parties have no realistic prospect of victory, there is the temptation for them to merge with a major party in return for whatever concessions can be gained (Key, 1964:274).

Independent state and local minor parties are also inhibited by the widespread practice of selecting local candidates through nonpartisan elections in which party labels are not printed on the ballot. The widespread use of the nonpartisan ballot in municipal elections was part of the reform movement of the late nineteenth and early twentieth centuries and was designed to weaken the hold of often corrupt party machines over city government. Interestingly, another motive for instituting the nonpartisan ballot was to thwart the new socialist parties that were electing mayors in various cities during the first two decades of the twentieth century. For example, in Wisconsin the legislature was persuaded to impose the nonpartisan ballot because it might prove useful in defeating a Socialist mayoral candidate in Milwaukee (Epstein, 1986:127).

As the earlier survey of party history in this chapter has shown, the most conspicuous minor parties have been national parties without significant state and local substructures. There have, however, been several minor parties of consequence that have existed on their local bases of support rather than as branches or offshoots of minor parties at the national level. In a few instances, these state-based minor parties achieved considerable success before either fading out or being absorbed into the major parties.

The Farmer-Labor Party of Minnesota

After unsuccessful attempts to operate as a faction within the dominant Minnesota Republican party, radical populist reformers created the Farmer-Labor party in the 1920s. By mobilizing hard-pressed farmers and laborers in the cities, it was able to become the principal opposition to the Republicans, as the Democrats had slipped into temporary limbo. Indeed, the Democratic party was largely absorbed into the Farmer-Labor party, and its percentage of the vote for governor fell to a mere 5.4 percent in 1926 (Sundquist, 1983:183). In 1930, the Farmer-Labor alliance scored a breakthrough, winning a clear majority for its gubernatorial candidate, Floyd B. Olson. The party continued to hold the office until 1938. In the 1940s, however, the pull of national political alignments overcame the Farmer-Labor party, and it suffered successive defeats. In 1944, the party merged with the Democrats to form the Democratic Farmer-Labor party (DFL), and the state resumed the conventional Republican-Democratic system of electoral competition. The DFL quickly became a power in state politics and sent Hubert H. Humphrey to the U.S. Senate in 1948. Humphrey was the first popularly elected Democratic senator in the state's history. In 1954, the DFL's nominee, Orville Freeman, took the governorship away from the Republicans.

La Follette's Progressive Party of Wisconsin

Like Minnesota, Wisconsin also experienced an interlude in the 1930s and 1940s when a third party became the principal opposition to the Republican party. For

more than two decades before the 1930s, meaningful electoral competition occurred within the Republican party between the conservative Stalwart faction and
the Progressives, led by the La Follette family. However, the Great Depression of
the 1930s discredited the Republican label, whether worn by a Stalwart or a Progressive. Facing reelection in 1934, Senator Robert M. La Follette Jr. was confronted with two obstacles. There was the distinct possibility that he could not
win the GOP primary against Stalwart opposition; only two years earlier, his
brother Philip had been defeated for the Republican gubernatorial nomination.
And even if he did succeed in winning the GOP primary, he would be running
with a party label that had lost much of its popular appeal due to the Depression.
In this situation, La Follette led his family's followers out of the Republican party
and formed the separate Progressive party of Wisconsin.

From 1934 to 1946, Wisconsin had three parties contesting elections in which the
most meaningful competition took place mainly between the Republicans and Progressives. With the departure of its Progressive faction, the Republican party came
to be dominated by conservatives. The Progressives became the liberal element in
state politics. La Follette and his followers supported Roosevelt's New Deal politics
and were the temporary beneficiaries of administration patronage and Democratic
National Committee backing. The state Democratic party was restricted to a narrow ethnic base—a coalition of conservative Irish, Polish, and German Catholics.

As in Minnesota, the tides of national politics swept over Wisconsin to the
detriment of the Progressives. Liberal and labor elements attracted by national
Democratic policies started to move into the state Democratic party. This movement was aided by Roosevelt's fourth-term candidacy, popular support for Democratic internationalism, and opposition to Progressive isolationism. In 1944,
with Roosevelt heading the Democrats' national ticket, no La Follette on the ballot, and a popular Republican governor, their vote fell to only 5.8 percent. Caught
between the emerging Democratic party and a strong Republican party whose
prospects looked particularly good in 1946, Senator La Follette concluded that his
best hope for reelection was as a Republican. Therefore, he sought the GOP senatorial nomination. However, he was defeated by Joseph M. McCarthy, who went
on to win the general election. La Follette's decision to enter the Republican primary and his loss to McCarthy killed the Progressive party, which never had a
strong organizational base and had always been heavily dependent upon the La
Follette family's personal following.

Although many Progressives in metropolitan areas did not follow their leaders
back into the Republican party, the return of many older and rural Progressives to
the GOP helped the Republicans maintain their electoral dominance in the state
for another decade. The demise of the Progressives did, however, result in many
rank-and-file Progressives shifting allegiance to the Democratic party. Since the

collapse of the Progressive party, electoral alignment in Wisconsin's state elections has been roughly congruent with its alignment in national elections.

The Nonpartisan League

The Nonpartisan League (NPL), which was once a major force in the politics of a triangle of states extending from Wisconsin to Oklahoma to Washington, provides another illustration of the survival problems of insurgent groups facing major parties that have remarkable capacities for absorption. The NPL was an organization of radical agrarian reform; it called for state ownership of grain elevators, flour mills, packing plants, mortgage banks, and hail insurance.

The NPL operated not as a political party but as a faction within the established parties. Its strategy was to "bore from within" by supporting candidates in the primaries. Between 1916 and 1922, it elected more than 950 candidates to state and federal offices (Key, 1964:278). Its greatest successes were in North Dakota, where between 1916 and 1919 it controlled the state legislature and statewide offices. The NPL declined after 1921 except in North Dakota, where it operated as a disciplined faction within the dominant Republican party until the 1950s. Younger liberal activists within the NPL, who had become restive operating within the GOP, and the liberal North Dakota Farmers Union then managed to take control of the NPL and merged it into the Democratic party in 1956, thereby creating a competitive two-party system within the state.

Multiparty Politics in New York State

The demise of the Farmer-Labor and Progressive parties as independent state parties in Minnesota and Wisconsin, and the merging of the NPL of North Dakota into the Democratic party, illustrate how national electoral alignments can overwhelm even relatively successful state-based minor parties. These cases also demonstrate the absorptive capacities of the major parties. The enduring nature of New York's multiparty system is, therefore, unique.

A major reason for the Empire State's distinctive party system is a type of election law that enhances the status of minor parties and effectively institutionalizes them. New York permits candidates to receive the nomination of more than one party and for candidates' names to appear on the ballot under the label of more than one party. This "cross-filing," or "fusion ticket," provision encouraged leaders of the heavily Jewish garment-industry unions in New York City to create the Liberal party of New York state in the 1940s as a way for garment workers to cast their ballots for Franklin D. Roosevelt, the Democratic nominee for president, while also voting against the candidates of the Democrats' Tammany Hall machine for other offices. For the Democrats in the 1950s and 1960s, victory and defeat frequently hinged upon the Liberal party vote. Thus, in 1954 Averell Harriman won the governorship by the narrowest of margins—50.1 percent of the vote—with 5.2 percent being supplied by citizens who cast votes for him using the Liberal line on the ballot. Similarly, in 1960 John F. Kennedy carried New York against Richard Nixon with 52.5 percent of the vote because he received 406,000 votes (5.6 percent) on the Liberal party line.

With the potential to determine election outcomes, the Liberal party gained substantial leverage within the Democratic party as it pressured Democratic leaders to nominate candidates acceptable to Liberal party voters. If the Democrats failed to nominate a candidate to their liking, the Liberal party had the option of nominating the Republican candidate or running its own candidate; either way, critical votes would be siphoned from the Democratic candidate.

Conservative Republicans, who were unhappy with their party's nominating liberals like Governor Nelson Rockefeller and Senator Jacob Javits, watched the Liberal party's efforts to blackmail the Democrats and decided that two could play that game. Disaffected right-wing Republicans in 1962 formed the Conservative party of New York state in an effort to exert influence upon Republican nominating politics.

With two major parties and a minor party allied with each of the major parties, Empire State politics has a unique character that can produce intense inter- and intraparty maneuvering and intrigue, not to mention unusual outcomes. In this Byzantine environment, it is even possible for a minor party to win a major office. For example, in the 1970 Senate election, the Republicans nominated former representative Charles Goodell, who had been appointed to fill the vacancy created by the assassination of Senator Robert F. Kennedy. Goodell had been a moderate conservative in the House of Representatives but adopted a liberal policy stance as a senator. As a result of this conversion, the Liberal party also gave him its nomination. The Democrats nominated a candidate from the party's mainstream, Representative Richard Ottinger. Meanwhile, the Conservative party rejected Goodell and instead selected as its candidate James Buckley, the brother of the well-known conservative columnist William F. Buckley. Republican operatives of President Richard Nixon and Governor Rockefeller then signaled that it was okay for Republicans to support Buckley. Vice President Spiro Agnew even attended a Buckley dinner, where he called Goodell the "Christine Jorgensen of the Republican party" (Jorgensen had just had a well-publicized sex-change operation). With the normal Democratic-Liberal vote split between Goodell (24 percent) and Ottinger (37 percent), Buckley, the Conservative nominee, was elected to the Senate with only 39 percent of the vote. However, when the minor parties were more conventionally aligned with their natural major party partners in 1982, Buckley lost his reelection bid to Democrat Daniel Patrick Moynihan, the Democratic-Liberal candidate.

In 1980, the alignment of the minor parties again affected the Senate election in a major way. Sensing that the ailing and liberal Republican incumbent, Jacob Javits, was vulnerable in a GOP primary, Alphonse D'Amato successfully challenged him for the Republican nomination; D'Amato also received the Conservative nomination. The Liberal party, however, remained loyal to Javits and placed him on the ballot as its nominee, leaving the Democratic candidate, New York City comptroller Elizabeth Holzman, without the customary Liberal line of the ballot. With the Democratic-Liberal vote split (44 percent for Holzman, 11 percent for Javits), D'Amato was able to enter the Senate with 45 percent of the vote.

As dramatic as these examples are of minor parties' impact on elections, the importance of the Liberal and Conservative parties should not be overstated. Normally, the Conservatives nominate the Republican candidate and the Liberals nominate a Democrat, or these minor parties refrain from putting up a candidate.[2] In addition, the Liberal party is declining as the number of Jewish garment workers in New York City shrinks. Thus, whereas John Kennedy gained 406,000 votes in 1960 on the Liberal line, Al Gore got only 77,087 in 2000. As the editors of the *Almanac of American Politics* have concluded, "The minor parties matter now only when they put on the ballot a candidate with specific appeal or a separate candidate to hurt a major party" (Barone and Ujifusa, 1993:864). However, the former has not happened since the Conservatives nominated James Buckley in 1970, and the latter has not occurred since D'Amato's election in 1980.

The Rarity of Seriously Contending Minor Parties in State Politics

In 1990, Walter Hickel, former governor of Alaska, and Lowell Weicker, former U.S. senator from Connecticut, both Republicans, were elected to their states' governorship on minor party tickets. However, when Hickel and Weicker declined to seek reelection, their new parties ceased to be major electoral forces within their states. In Maine, Angus King, an independent, captured the governor's mansion in 1994 and was reelected in 1998. Unlike Hickel and Weicker, King never sought to form and lead a state-level political party. Therefore, Maine politics continues to be dominated by the Republicans and the Democrats. The inability of these prominent politicians to fashion permanent state-based parties illustrates the extent to which state politics is dominated by the major parties. Even in New York, where election laws bestow special protection to minor parties, their influence appears to be declining.

The party-building activities of Minnesota's Jesse Ventura provide further evidence of just how difficult it is to create a viable state-level third party. In 1998, the former professional wrestler and suburban mayor became the first Reform party candidate to be elected to statewide office when he upset the incumbent Democratic attorney general and the Republican mayor of St. Paul with populist, straight-talking rhetoric, a tough-guy image, and publicity-generating showmanship. His low-budget campaign benefited from Minnesota's public financing law, which provided Ventura's campaign with $400,000 while limiting the expenditures of the major party candidates who (having also accepted public fundings) were restricted to spending only $2.1 million each. In spite of his dramatic 1998 victory, Ventura has not been successful in building a viable state-level party. He left the Reform party amid its bitter 2000 presidential nomination contest and sought to create the Minnesota Independence party. In the 2000 election, the new Ventura-founded party was not able to recruit a full slate of candidates and fared badly at the polls. As with other non-major party governors elected in the 1990s, Ventura faced a legislature dominated by the two major parties.

Seriously contending minor parties are not a standard feature of American state politics. The few state-based minor parties that have had some electoral success recently all proved unable to sustain themselves against the pull of national electoral alignments and the absorptive capacities of the Republican and Democratic parties. Today, minor parties are more likely to play a spoiler role, as the example of the special election in New Mexico, with the Green party taking votes away from Democratic House candidates (noted in Chapter 1), demonstrates.

Lessons from Party History

This brief survey of party history demonstrates one of the most salient and enduring features of the American political system: the durability and institutionalized nature of the two-party system. It also documents the stability of Democratic-Republican electoral dominance. Since the 1850s, the same two parties have confronted each other as the major combatants in the electoral arena. Each has sustained and suffered dramatic swings of fortune—landslide victories, demoralizing defeats, cliffhanger wins and losses, major splinter movements, and realignments of bases for electoral support. Despite the fluidity of voting patterns over the decades and political dislocations created by two world wars, depressions, waves of new immigrants, industrialization, urbanization, globalization, and changes in lifestyles, the Republican-Democratic two-party system endures.

History also reveals that third-party movements and independent candidacies have been a consistent and integral component of the two-party system. As Walter

Dean Burnham has observed, third-party protests have often been a "proto-realignment phenomenon" that occurred before major electoral realignments and reflected the inability of the existing major parties to meet the expectations of large segments of society. Thus, the Anti-Masonic party preceded the emergence of the Democratic-Whig party system; the Free Soil party rose prior to the collapse of the Whigs and the emergence of the Republicans; the Populist uprising in 1892 took place before the McKinley-Bryan realigning election of 1896; and the La Follette Progressive party of 1924 foreshadowed the rise of the New Deal Democratic coalition (Burnham, 1970). Similarly, the Dixiecrat revolt and George Wallace's candidacy were precursors of the post–New Deal party system.

Third-party and independent candidates have also helped to push issues onto the public agenda when the major parties were unwilling to confront them: Free Soilers on the slavery issue; Perot on budget deficits in 1992. The argument that third parties advocate and build public support for policies that the major parties are then forced to adopt, however, can be overstated. It is argued, for example, that the Socialist party's twenty-five-year advocacy of such policies as the minimum wage led to the policy being adopted during the Roosevelt administration. However, as Paul Allen Beck has pointed out, "Unfortunately, there is no way of testing what might have happened had there been no Socialist party. The evidence suggests, however, that major parties grasp new programs and proposals in their 'time of ripeness' when large numbers of Americans have done so and when such a course is therefore politically useful to the parties" (1997:49).

It should also be noted that new issues do not depend solely on minor parties for publicity and advocacy. As Beck has further noted, "Interest groups, the mass media, influential individuals, and factions within the major parties may perform the propagandizing role, often more effectively than a minor party. More than one commentator has noted that the cause of prohibition . . . was served far more effectively by interest groups such as the Anti-Saloon League than the Prohibition party" (1997:49).

Although third parties and independent candidates are a recurring phenomenon of the American party system and have even significantly affected the outcome of elections, the hard fact remains that since the 1850s, only one new party—the Republican party—has moved on to achieve major party status. More than 145 years of Democratic-Republican two-partyism thus raises the question of why third-party movements have not emerged to seriously challenge or replace either major party, as in the United Kingdom, Western Europe, and Canada. In Chapter 3 we explore this basic question, examining a variety of historical, cultural, and institutional factors.

3

....

Third Parties in the American Context: A Less Than Friendly Environment

As this demonstrator is showing, Democrats feared that Green party nominee Ralph Nader would take needed votes away from Al Gore in 2000.

THE FACT THAT THE United States has the oldest and strongest two-party system on the globe is, for many, particularly foreign observers, a bewildering phenomenon. America appears to have all the ingredients for a vibrant and enduring multiparty system—an increasingly multiracial and multiethnic population, substantial regional variation, diverse and conflicting economic and social interests, a history of sectional conflicts, and substantial disparities in the distribution of wealth. Why, then, is two-party politics so entrenched, both nationally and at the state level?

A political system dominated by two parties certainly has not come about because the nation's founders envisioned an enduring system of that nature in their grand design for the republic; to the contrary, they sought to create a system that would preclude party development (recall the passage from Washington's Farewell Address quoted in Chapter 2). Neither is the two-party system's survival due to its having gained the public's overwhelming affection. For instance, a 1995 Gallup Poll showed that almost two-thirds of the public thought "the more the merrier" when indicating support for the creation of a new independent party (Moore, 1996:1). That sentiment was again present in the run-up to the 2000 elections. The Gallup Poll reported in July 1999 that 67 percent of those surveyed wanted a strong third party that could run candidates against the Republicans and Democrats for president, Congress, and state offices. By the summer of 2000, when many voters had begun to feel a resurgence of partisanship, slightly more than a majority of Americans (52 percent) still said that the nation should have a third major party ("Third Party Sentiment Waxes and Wanes," 2000).

Yet it is not just the public that currently has doubts about two-party hegemony. Opinion leaders are also questioning the desirability, or at least the viability, of the existing Republican-Democratic system. Theodore Lowi, former president of the American Political Science Association, has been particularly outspoken in his condemnation of two-partyism as it operates in the United States. He has asserted that the two-party system is "brain dead," with Republican and Democratic parties "immobilized by having to promise too many things to too many people." Lowi went on to charge that the existing parties are undemocratic in that they resist leadership change, fail to bring new issues to the fore, avoid critical issues, preserve a protective institutional structure, and stifle competition

(Lowi, 1996). The *Washington Post*'s respected correspondent David Broder even went so far as to predict the demise of one or both major parties if they did not resolve the nation's looming entitlement crises in Social Security and Medicare within eighteen months of the 1996 elections (Broder 1996).

In spite of weak public support and the critical assessments of the system by some respected observers, the collapse of the two-party system does not appear likely in the foreseeable future. We are, therefore, left with a dilemma: how to account for the development and durability of the American two-party system.

Why Two Major Parties and Not a Multiparty System?

There is no single explanation for dualism in the American party system. Rather, a combination of factors has encouraged its development and still contributes to its maintenance. This combination of influences includes special historical circumstances, public attitudes, and institutional arrangements and procedures governing elections.

Historical Conditions

The special circumstances of the initial political conflicts in the new republic and the tendency for human institutions to perpetuate themselves and preserve their initial form bear some responsibility for the current existence of the two-party system. The initial confrontation that the new nation faced was the issue of ratification of the Constitution, a yes-no issue that tended to polarize national opinion. The small farmers and debtors of the interior regions were pitted against the mercantile and financial interests on the East Coast. The initial lines of cleavage were built upon a dualism of interests—agricultural interests and financial-mercantile interests—during an era when the economic and social structure of the country was far less complex than it is today. Partisan conflict thus began in an era characterized by a dualist cleavage. The pattern of two-party politics continued, however, even though the society and economy changed substantially. As V. O. Key Jr. has observed:

> The great issues changed from time to time but each party managed to renew itself as it found new followers to replace those it lost. The Civil War thus brought a realignment of national politics, yet it re-enforced the dual division. For decades southern Democrats recalled the heroes of the Confederacy and the Republicans waved the "bloody shirt" to rally their followers. As memories of the war faded new alignments gradually took shape within the matrix of the preexisting structure, with each party hierarchy struggling to maintain its position in the system. (1964:208)

Indeed, as Americans enter the twenty-first century, the two major parties have gone through another significant electoral realignment, one that finds white Southerners predominantly in the Republican camp, black voters overwhelmingly loyal to the Democrats, a growing Hispanic population voting heavily Democratic, Catholics no longer strongly committed to the Democrats, women voters siding with the Democrats, men favoring the GOP, and regular church attendees tending toward the GOP, whereas the unchurched are apt to vote Democratic.

Systems of Beliefs and Attitudes

Political dualism in the United States has been facilitated by the pattern of popular political beliefs and attitudes among the citizenry. American society is not characterized by blocs of people irreconcilably attracted to a particular ideology or creed. Racial, religious, and ethnic minorities, though often feeling the sting of discrimination, have not tended toward separatism or extremism. Religious tensions have existed, but open conflict has never been commonplace, and First Amendment protections have generally been observed. Neither has America developed the degree of class-consciousness that can be found in Europe. Labor parties have had little appeal to American workers, male or female. There is virtually universal acceptance and support for the existing constitutional order and a capitalist economic system.

So even though diversity flourishes within American society, there has been a general absence of groups so committed to a cause that they could not be accommodated within one of the major parties. No group is seeking to restore the prerogatives of the church as a state religion; no major group is seriously advocating socialism or monarchy; a labor party would have few adherents; no one is seriously calling for racially, ethnically, or regionally based political parties. Should such groups exist in significant numbers, multiparty politics would be possible.

The attitudes that undergird a system of political dualism do not rely solely on the absence of blocs of citizens with irreconcilable parochial beliefs. As Key noted, there is a pattern of attitudes in the United States that favors political dualism, even though its precise nature remains somewhat elusive.

> It is often described as a popular consensus on fundamentals. Powerful mechanisms of education and indoctrination, along with accidents of history, maintain broad agreement . . . upon political essentials. At times, it can be said, with a color of truth, that we are all liberals; at another time, it may be equally true that we are all conservatives. *Given this tendency for most people to cluster fairly closely together in their attitudes, a dual division becomes possible.* (1964:210, emphasis added)

Extremists do exist in the American context, but their numbers are relatively small, and they stand far outside the central mode of public opinion. Therefore, given the broad agreement that exists among the citizenry, it is possible for the policy preferences of one party to be slightly left of center or liberal, for those of the other to be slightly right of center or conservative, and for each to gain broad-based electoral support. Thus, the Democrats and Republicans can attract divergent cores of support that have quite different policy preferences and can still compete for the vote of the vast majority of Americans who consider themselves middle-of-the-roaders. For example, among the keys to Bill Clinton's electoral success was his ability to hold his party's core supporters (e.g., blacks, union members) while also moving the Democratic party toward a position where it was viewed as more centrist than it had been in the 1970s and 1980s, when it lost White House bids with nominees George McGovern, Walter Mondale, and Michael Dukakis, each of whom was strongly identified with the party's liberal wing. Similarly in 2000, George W. Bush, by stressing his theme of "compassionate conservatism," was able to project a relatively centrist Republican image without alienating his conservative base.

Institutional Barriers to Multiparty Politics

A variety of institutional arrangements in the United States operates to encourage and perpetuate the two-party system and frustrate the aspirations of parties that would challenge Republican-Democratic dominance. Some of these institutional arrangements command widespread public backing and are so firmly established in the American political culture that it is hard to imagine their being rearranged to benefit third parties in the foreseeable future.

The Single-Member, Plurality, District System

The standard arrangement for electing U.S. senators and representatives, as well as state legislators, is **the single-member district system**, in which whoever wins a plurality of votes is elected. In this system, there are no rewards for coming in second, third, or fourth; there is only one winning party per district. By contrast, in countries utilizing **proportional representation** systems, all serious parties are rewarded with legislative seats in proportion to their share of the total vote. Proportional representation schemes thus set up incentives for the creation and perpetuation of multiple and distinct parties. Often, these parties have relatively narrow or pure policy positions and do not attempt to win broad-based support. However, in a proportional representation system, minor parties can still win legislative seats in proportion to their total vote even though they receive only a small share of the popular vote. In short, proportional representation schemes create incentives to form and maintain a wide variety of parties designed to appeal to various special interests in society, whereas systems with plurality-winner, single-member districts do not.

In contrast to the proportional representation system, the single-member district system (dubbed by the British "first-past-the-post") creates a very different set of political incentives. Permitting as it does only one party to win in any given legislative district, the single-member system brings with it incentives toward the creation of two broadly based parties that are capable of winning district-level pluralities and majorities in the legislative chamber. In a single-member district system, third and minor parties are normally condemned to almost perpetual defeat—not a prescription for longevity—unless they can combine forces with one of the larger parties.

The single-member district system can be a powerful influence in encouraging two-partyism (Neto and Cox, 1997). However, the experience of the United Kingdom and Canada—both of which use first-past-the-post systems yet still have multiparty systems—demonstrates that this institutional arrangement can only encourage, not necessitate, two-party competition. The single-member district system cannot ensure two-partyism when there is a high level of social heterogeneity undergirding the political system. Thus, in Canada—with its concentration of French-speaking voters in Quebec, Westerners harboring a strong sense of alienation from the central government, and the presence of a social democratic movement—the single-member district system is not a barrier to multiparty politics. In the 2000 parliamentary elections, two parties (the Liberals and the Reform Alliance) gained more than 25 percent of the vote, two received in excess of 10 percent (Bloc Quebecois and the Progressive Conservatives), and the New Democrats got nine percent.

The Separation of Powers System

A chief executive elected separately from the national legislature with a term that overlaps that of the upper- and lower-chamber legislators—as is true of the American system—creates an incentive to create broad-based parties capable of winning the grand prize of the political system—the presidency. Again, this incentive contrasts with the situation in a parliamentary system, in which coalitions are built in the legislature after an election in order to form a government and choose those who serve as executives. The incentives to form two broad-based parties with a realistic chance of winning the presidency are especially strong when the chief executive is chosen via a system that requires pluralities of the popular votes in a large number of individual states, as is the case with the American Electoral College system (Abramson et al., 1995).

The Electoral College System

The Electoral College system for electing presidents provides an additional nudge toward two-party competition. The Constitution requires an absolute majority of the electoral votes (at least 270 out of 538 total) for a candidate to be elected president. This requirement makes it most unlikely that a third party can ever achieve the presidency without combining with or absorbing one of the major parties. Third parties are further disadvantaged by the fact that all but two states (Maine and Nebraska) allocate their electoral votes to candidates on a **winner-take-all** basis.[1] All that is required to win all of a state's electoral votes is a plurality of the vote in that state. Like the single-member district system, the winner-take-all feature of the Electoral College means that third parties have little chance of winning any state's electoral votes, let alone carrying a sufficient number of states to elect a president.

Ross Perot's 1992 campaign is illustrative of the difficulties posed by the Electoral College system. He gained a respectable 18.9 percent of the popular vote, but he did not win a plurality in a single state and thus ended up with no electoral votes whatsoever. Regionally based candidates such as George Wallace in 1968 or Populist James Weaver in 1892 had sufficiently concentrated support in selected states to win a small number of electoral votes. But regional candidates lack the broad-based appeal of the major parties that is essential to gain an Electoral College majority.

Although most third parties are normally unable to win a significant share of the electoral vote under the Electoral College's winner-take-all system for allocating a state's electoral votes, this does not mean that they can have no impact on the outcome. As was noted in Chapter 2, Ralph Nader's Green party candidacy in 2000 arguably prevented Al Gore from carrying such closely contested states as Florida, New Hampshire, and Tennessee, thereby helping George W. Bush gain a majority in the Electoral College.

The Direct Primary System for Nominating Congressional and State Officials

One of the reasons for the unprecedented Democratic-Republican electoral dominance for over 145 years has been the **direct primary** system for nominating candidates to run for congressional and state offices. Primary elections, which allow voters to select party candidates directly, are a uniquely American institution. The pervasive use of this system in all fifty states has channeled dissent into the two major parties. In the United States, unlike in other nations, dissidents and insurgents do not need to go through the difficult and often frustrating exercise of forming an alternative party. Instead, they can work within the Republican or Democratic party by seeking to win major party nominations as a route to elective office. This "burrowing from within" strategy is much more likely to yield success than the third-party or independent candidacy method.

The direct primary makes American parties particularly porous and susceptible to external influences and in the process reduces incentives to create additional parties. The porous and nondoctrinaire character of American major parties also enables them readily to absorb protest movements (e.g., the Democrats absorbed the Populists in 1896; the Democrats took back the 1948 Dixiecrats; the Republicans and Democrats sought the followers of George Wallace after 1968; and both parties openly courted Perot voters of 1992 and 1996).

The impact of the direct primary is thus paradoxical. On the one hand, the primary system has weakened American parties organizationally by taking from party leaders control over one of the parties' most important functions: the selection of candidates. On the other hand, the electoral looseness that the primary system imposes upon the parties acts as a party preservative and helps enable the major parties to absorb protest movements and dissidents. Through the direct primary, voters have become accustomed to choosing among groups and individuals competing for the Republican or Democratic label. In addition, a substantial number of states require voters to register as Democrats or Republicans in order to participate in primary elections. Allegiance to party is thus institutionalized by state law or party rules. All of these aspects of the direct primary system have thus helped to institutionalize Democratic-Republican electoral dominance (Epstein, 1986: 244–245).

The Presidential Primary System

Just as the direct primary encourages insurgents to work from within the two major parties, so does the presidential primary system for nominating major party candidates. Insurgents out of step with party leadership can use presidential primaries to seek the nomination and press their claims within the party (e.g., Democrats George Wallace in 1964, 1968, and 1972, Eugene McCarthy in 1968, Jesse Jackson in 1984, and Bill Bradley in 2000; and Republicans John Anderson in 1980, Pat Buchanan in 1992 and 1996, and John McCain in 2000). Up until 1972, the presidential nominating process had been an anomaly in that party leaders were able to exert a powerful and often determining influence over the selection of presidential nominees.

The post-1968 reforms initiated by the Democrats opened up the system to mass participation and a proliferation of presidential primaries that have taken control of nominations out of the hands of party leaders and transferred it to primary voters. These post-1968 changes have had the effect of bringing presidential nominations into rough conformity with the way nominations for other partisan offices are decided—using the direct primary. The consequences of having primaries decide presidential nominations have been similar to the effects of the direct primary system—dissidents and insurgents use the primaries of existing major parties to achieve their goals rather than opting for the more difficult task of forming an alternative party (Epstein, 1993:152).

The direct primary was a Progressive Era reform that is now firmly entrenched in the American political culture. Also widely accepted is the participatory nature of presidential nominating politics, made possible because a majority of the states select their delegates to the national conventions using presidential primaries. Indeed, voter participation in nominations is now such an accepted part of the American political system that no realistic political leader can suggest that primaries should or could be replaced by procedures that would put party leaders back in control of candidate selection. This reality dims the prospects for a strong alternative to the Democrats or Republicans emerging anytime soon.

Public Funding of Election Campaigns

Advocates of a multiparty system are certainly correct in asserting that the Federal Election Campaign Act functions in a manner that benefits the two major parties at the expense of minor parties. Under the FECA, a party is eligible for public funding of its candidate's presidential campaign, provided that the party's nominee in the previous presidential election received the requisite percentage of the popular vote. Major parties—defined under the law as those that received at least 25 percent of the vote in the last presidential election—are entitled to full funding ($67.6 million in 2000) of their candidates' general election campaigns. Minor parties can receive a much smaller allocation of federal funds if they meet the minimum requirement of 5 percent of the vote in the previous election.

Since it is difficult to imagine a set of circumstances in which the Republican and Democratic presidential candidates do not receive at least one-fourth of the vote, the FECA, in effect, seems to guarantee the two major parties a government-subsidized existence in perpetuity. By contrast, even third parties that qualify for public funding do so at a much lower level than the major parties. Thus, the Democratic and Republican nominees in 2000 received a public subsidy of $67.6 million, whereas Pat Buchanan (the Reform party nominee) got $12.6 million. FECA also assists the major parties by funding their national conventions with public funds and providing matching money to their candidates during the preconvention presidential primaries and state party caucuses to select national convention delegates.

When the constitutionality of FECA was challenged in the case of *Buckley v. Valeo* (1976), the U.S. Supreme Court demonstrated its willingness to distinguish between major and minor parties and support a two-party system. It recognized Congress's interest in not squandering taxpayers' money to fund hopeless candidates and accepted the legitimacy of an important national interest against providing artificial incentives to "splintered and unrestrained factionalism." The Court also took notice of the fact that throughout American history, except for the elections of 1856 and 1860, when the Republicans replaced the Whigs, "no third party has posed a credible threat to the two major parties in presidential elections." It said that "Congress was aware of this fact of American life, and thus was justified in providing both major parties full funding and all the other parties only a percentage of the major-party entitlement" (see commentary of Peltason, 1999:20–23).

Because all the minor parties running candidates for president in 2000 failed to garner at least 5 percent of the vote, none qualified for public funding in 2004. By winning well in excess of the required 25 percent of the 2000 vote, the Republican and Democratic parties, of course, qualified for the maximum amount of public money in 2004. The grants to the major parties will be adjusted to account for inflation. As a result, the public funding that will be made available to the Republican and Democratic nominees in 2004 will exceed the $67.6 million given in 2000.

Minor parties are not as clearly disadvantaged under—and some claim they may be helped by—so-called clean election laws that have been passed by several states. Such laws provide public funding for major- as well as minor-party candidates. Minnesota, Vermont, and Maine are notable examples. Candidates for governor and other state offices—including minor- and major-party candidates—may qualify for full public funding, including funding for primary campaigns, provided that they raise a certain amount of money in small donations, reach a qualifying threshold, and pledge to abide by strict caps on spending.

In Minnesota in 1998, Jesse Ventura benefited from the state's public-funding law. The 1998 Reform party candidate qualified for $400,000 in public funding by winning 5 percent of the vote in the primary. With his public funds, Ventura moved beyond being a marginal candidate and was able to run comical and irreverent radio and TV ads, including one that featured Jesse "The Body" Ventura posing as Rodin's *The Thinker*. Ventura's campaign theatrics and populist style generated additional (free) media coverage; and he was included in televised debates alongside the major party candidates. In this way he became a serious contender.

Ventura's Republican and Democratic opponents also qualified for—and accepted—public funding, but they were required by accepting public money to limit their expenditures to $2.1 million. As a result of this limitation—and because they did not realize the electoral threat posed by Ventura until late in the campaign, by which time each had nearly reached the spending limit—they were prevented from bombarding the voters with TV ads to counter those Ventura ran in the closing weeks and days of the campaign. Thus, the public money for which Ventura qualified—combined with the spending restrictions placed on the major party candidates' campaigns because of both law and their strategic budget decisions—contributed to the viability and eventual success of his relatively low budget, publicly funded, minor party campaign (Jeter, 1998; see also Lentz 2002).

In Vermont in the 2000 election, the Progressive party gubernatorial candidate qualified for $300,000 in public funding. To offset the advantages of incumbency, Vermont law allows incumbent governors to receive only $225,000 in public funds and limits their spending to that amount (Goldberg, 2000). Vermont has elected Bernie Sanders, an independent whose campaigns have sparked interest in Progressive party politics, to the U.S. House of Representatives for several terms. As the state has only one congressional district, Sanders's organization has spanned the state. Although the Progressive gubernatorial candidate did not win in 2000, his campaign was viable because public funding added legitimacy, allowed it to reach more voters, and gave some of Sanders's more liberal supporters another option.

In Maine, the Green party has two "clean candidates" (those who accept public funding and thereby agree to spending caps) in the 2002 gubernatorial primary. The Maine law calls for dividing the amount spent in the previous election cycle on a parallel campaign among qualifying clean candidates. Thus, the two Green party candidates will each receive approximately $120,000 to run their campaigns. (Only one of the candidates in the major party primaries is running as a clean candidate. The others must abide by a limit on the size of donations but are not restricted by an overall spending limit. The public money is divided among the clean candidates, any one of whom can receive additional money if an opponent exceeds the imposed limit in spending.) Maine is a closed primary state with only 8,000 or so registered Green party members, so the two candidates will each be able to spend about $15 per voter. More realistically, they will be able to use the money to build the Green party's base and to enroll new party members.

Critics fear clean campaign laws will make public funding easier to obtain and thus lead to more and more minor party candidates on the ballot. Supporters do not disagree but feel that such candidacies deserve support. In elections held under such laws thus far, the number of minor party candidates has not dramatically increased, but the experience is too recent for any trend to be noted.

National Nominating Conventions

Although the major TV networks no longer provide gavel-to-gavel coverage of national conventions because presidential primaries, and not the conventions, actually determine the nominees, the conventions continue to be political events that command media coverage—hence the parties' careful staging of their conventions and their vigorous attempts to avoid images of divisiveness that might drive away voters. The conventions' impact on the electorate's preferences can be substantial. For example, in 1992 Bill Clinton got a 13.6 percent "bump" in the polls following his party's highly successful convention, and George Bush gained 8.4 percent in the polls after the 1988 GOP convention (Holbrook, 1996:79). The 2000 conventions also benefited the major party nominees. George W. Bush received a four percent point bounce in the Gallup Poll from the coverage he received during the Republican convention as he increased his lead over Al Gore in the polls to 16 percentage points. The Democratic convention provided an even greater bounce for the Gore candidacy. Polls taken after the convention showed the race to be a dead heat as Gore gained strength, particularly among women, and the convention stimulated more Democrats to say they would vote in the November elections (Moore, 2000).

Postconvention "bumps" in the polls due to favorable images in the national media, however, are the exclusive property of the major parties. Third parties rarely have the resources to stage national conventions on a scale that can compete with the four-day, prime-time television productions of the Republicans and Democrats. The third parties' disadvantage in media coverage was clearly evident in 1996. Attention to the new Reform party's convention was eclipsed by the news media's focus upon the Republican convention. Bob Dole, the Republican nominee, received extensive free news media coverage, particularly for his selection of Jack Kemp to be his vice presidential running mate. By contrast, Ross Perot had to pay CBS for a half-hour of network time to announce his choice for vice president, Washington economist Pat Choate (Nagourney, 1996).

The story played out the same for the Reform party in 2000. Its convention generated little media coverage, and the coverage it did receive was anything but positive. For example, the *New York Times* relegated the Reform convention to page 20 of its Sunday, August 13, national edition with the headline A CONVEN-TION ENDS AS BITTERLY AS IT BEGAN, WITH RIVAL NOMINEES AND A LIKELY LAWSUIT. The article featured a photo of a disgruntled delegate; the article began with an unflattering lead sentence: "Battered and sundered into competing factions, the Reform Party fought through the final hours of a bitter national convention today, then limped out of town as two parties, each with its own ideology and nominee" (Ayres and Janofsky, 2000).

Presidential Debates

The ultimate prize of American electoral politics is control of the presidency. Since becoming institutionalized, the televised **presidential debates** have become major events in the campaign. The debates generate heavy media coverage and bestow legitimacy upon the candidates who take part. The major party candidates are automatically invited to spar with each other in these debates. Minor party and independent candidates, however, are not assured of a right to participate.

Control over who gets to take part is in the hands of the ten-member bipartisan Commission on Presidential Debates, which is cochaired by former chairmen of the Democratic and Republican National Committees. In 1996, the commission barred Ross Perot, the Reform party nominee, from participating. The commission made that decision after consulting with an advisory panel chaired by a distinguished political scientist, Richard A. Neustadt, concluding that Ross Perot did not meet the commission's criteria for participation: He did not have a "realistic chance" of winning the election. A federal district court upheld the commission's decision to exclude Perot, stating that courts do not have the power to determine who should participate in the debates and that candidates have no constitutional right to do so. The court did acknowledge, however, that the procedures governing participation had led to "frustration and perhaps unfairness for those who consider themselves legitimate candidates."

Third parties faced a similar fate in the 2000 presidential debates. The commission formulated a new criterion that candidates must meet in order to participate. This new requirement, which neither Pat Buchanan of the Reform party nor Ralph Nader of the Greens could meet, stated that candidates must receive 15 percent in five national polls to be included in the debates. Paul G. Kirk Jr., the former Democratic National Chairman who cochairs the commission with former Republican National Chairman Frank Fahrenhopf, responded when Buchanan and Nader alleged that they could not win if they were shut out of the debates: "Our role is not to jump-start your campaign and all of a sudden make you competitive. . . . It's not a perfect analogy, but in sports, people understand you don't make the playoffs unless you start to accumulate enough wins to show you're competitive" ("Win Your Way to Playoffs, Debate Chair Says," 2000).

Even if a third-party or independent candidate is invited to take part, he might be boycotted by a major party candidate who fears the outsider will jeopardize his own chances. Thus, in 1980 President Jimmy Carter refused to participate in a three-way debate with the two other candidates, Republican Ronald Reagan and independent John B. Anderson. Carter was concerned that giving Anderson exposure would take away votes from his own candidacy. Hence, he agreed only to a two-way debate with Reagan.

The debates' format is always a contentious issue between the major parties' candidates, as various formats (e.g., questions from a panel of journalists; audience participation; or a single moderator with the candidates responding to each other) can favor the skills and style of one candidate over another. Normally, the debate format is decided through protracted and often contentious negotiations among the managers for the Republican and Democratic nominees, without much input from third-party or independent candidates (even when they are allowed to participate).

Difficulties in Gaining Media Coverage

Successful campaigns require continuing and prominent coverage by the news media. For most major party candidates, this type of coverage is almost automatic. However, for third-party candidates, breaking into the media is an obstacle to building a base of support and raising what they consider legitimate issues.

The issue for many journalists is, why should a candidate who is never going to win deserve attention? Third-party and independent candidates are, therefore, plagued by the need to demonstrate viability and legitimacy. In 1980, for example, the *New York Times* reported that John Anderson at every campaign stop was asked to justify his presidential candidacy and answer the charge that he was merely a spoiler candidate (Smith, 1980). By contrast, the major party presidential nominees, Ronald Reagan and Jimmy Carter, never faced such questions.

When minor party candidates are covered in the media, the nature of that coverage has characteristics that work to the candidates' disadvantage. News stories about them are seldom front-page items and instead are buried in the back pages of newspapers and feature smaller-type headlines than the stories on Republican and Democratic candidates. Coverage tends to be in the form of analysis and critique rather than straight news, and there is disproportionate attention to personal characteristics of the candidates rather than their views on foreign and economic policy. Media stories almost universally focus on themes of failure, even farce. Witness the following headlines (Collet, 2001) from national newspapers in the 2000 campaign:

MOST MINOR PARTY CANDIDATES BARELY SEEN, KNOWN
(*USA Today*, November 7)

NADER, BUCHANAN REMAIN ON SIDELINES
(*Arizona Republic*, October 3)

3RD PARTY LAMENT: ANYONE LISTENING? IT'S NOT EASY BEING GREEN,
OR LIBERTARIAN, OR SOCIALIST (*New York Times*, October 25)

THIRD-PARTY CANDIDATES LEFT OUT IN THE COLD
(*Los Angeles Times*, October 4)

Clearly, the media's approach to third parties makes it extremely difficult to develop electoral strength in an environment dominated by the Democrats and the Republicans.

State Regulations and Ballot Access Laws

When examining the American party system, one must emphasize the federal nature of this polity. States make their own laws in many areas. Frequently, as is the case with election law, different states adopt different procedures. This very fact makes it difficult for those who favor a multiparty system to accomplish their end by changing national laws.

Even the states' much-heralded 1890s reform measure—the **Australian ballot**, whereby official government-printed ballots replaced those printed and distributed by political parties—had adverse consequences for minor parties seeking to challenge the major parties. As long as the parties provided ballots, it was possible for new parties to gain access to polling places and voters and thereby challenge the major parties. Indeed, a study of the Whig party in the pre–Civil War era reveals that new parties printing their own ballots were extremely effective in siphoning votes from the Whigs and contributed mightily to that party's demise. With new parties printing their own ballots, the Whigs could not monopolize opposition to the Democrats, as their Republican successors can today (Holt, 1999).

As noted previously, state-prescribed direct primary laws have aided Republicans and Democrats by discouraging special interests and other groups from seeking power by establishing new parties or strengthening existing minor parties. The major parties' nominees also gain an aura of democratic legitimacy in having their candidates selected through state-established primaries. In general, state laws regulating the electoral process impose additional legal burdens on new and minor parties, as well as on independent candidacies (Epstein, 1986:173). These requirements should not be surprising, for Republican and Democratic legislators write the laws governing elections. The Republican and Democratic parties are assured of automatic ballot access (having their parties' names and candidates on the general election ballot) because of their prior success in winning votes.

For new parties and independent candidates, however, ballot access is not automatic. They are required to submit petitions signed by a large number of voters just to get their candidates onto the ballot. The highest such hurdle was created by Pennsylvania in 1997. Had this law been in effect in 1996, a third party would have been required to secure more than 99,000 signatures on a petition during a fourteen-week period to gain ballot access for its presidential candidate (Seelye, 1997). In 2000, the Reform and Libertarian parties each had to obtain 51,324 signatures for their presidential candidates.

"Sore loser" laws also work to protect the two major parties in many states. Such laws are designed to keep those who lose primary elections from turning around and running in the general election as independents. If candidates were allowed to follow such a strategy, those without firm ties to political parties would have two chances at victory, whereas party loyalists would have only one. Sore loser laws have been upheld by the courts on the grounds that they protect the integrity of the electoral process. There is no question that these laws protect the major parties from fringe candidates who might try to capture major party nominations knowing they can always run as independents if they lose the first time around (Price, 1984:132–134). In upholding California's "sore loser" statute, the U.S. Supreme Court noted that states have a legitimate interest in preventing "splintered parties and unrestrained factionalism" within their borders (*Storer v. Brown*, 414 U.S. 737 [1974]; see also Peltason, 1999:19–20).

In 1997, the Supreme Court (see *Timmons v. Twin Cities Area New Party*, involving a left-leaning party in Minnesota) dealt minor parties a severe setback when it ruled that states can prohibit candidates from appearing on the ballot on more than one party's line. Such **"cross-filing,"** or **"fusion,"** is widely practiced in New York state, which allows candidates to place their names on the ballot as the nominee of more than one party. By permitting cross-filing, New York has encouraged minor parties and facilitated coalitions between Democrats and the Liberal party and between Republicans and the Conservative party. Because the Liberal and Conservative parties have substantial followings, their nominations can boost votes for major party nominees. However, the possibility that these parties might refuse to nominate their coalition partner's candidate and instead run their own candidate—or even nominate the other major party's candidate—can pose a serious threat to their coalition partner's electoral prospects. New York's cross-filing system has given the state a multiparty system and a nominating process filled with intrigue and subtle maneuvering among the parties that gives the Empire State a unique brand of politics (Scarrow, 1983:55–80).

In *Timmons*, the New party sought to nominate a state legislative candidate who had already accepted the Democratic nomination. Speaking for a six-judge majority, Chief Justice William H. Rehnquist noted that political parties have an unquestioned right to select their own candidates but that states also have the constitutional right to regulate elections to prevent manipulation of the ballot and factionalism among voters. The Court thus blessed the two-party system, stating that the "Constitution permits the Minnesota Legislature to decide that political stability is best served through a healthy two-party system" (Greenhouse, 1997).

Given that state laws can restrict ballot access and that a tolerant federal judiciary has upheld these restrictions, third parties and independent candidates operate in a less than hospitable legal environment (see Winger, 1995). It should be noted, however, that a number of states have been moving to ease ballot restrictions (Bass, 1996). Nonetheless, state laws have tended to create an "institutionalized electoral duopoly" (Epstein, 1986:173).

The Limits of Institutional Arrangements in Protecting Major Parties

The various institutional arrangements arrayed against third parties, minor parties, and independent candidates are indeed formidable. The combination of institutional arrangements described earlier has certainly encouraged the development and perpetuation of two-party politics in America as well as the long-term electoral dominance of the Republican and Democratic parties. However, America's unrivaled history of two-party politics should not obscure a basic political truth: "No electoral system protects major political parties from the electorate" (Abramson et al., 1995:366–367). The Progressive Conservatives (PCs) of Canada learned this lesson to their sorrow in 1993 when they went from being the majority party in the House of Commons to minor party status with only two legislative seats; and in succeeding national elections of 1997 and 2000, the PCs have failed to regain their former party status as the major opposition to the dominant Liberal party.

In spite of utilizing a single-member district system, Canada has a lively multiparty system. In Great Britain, which also uses the single-member district system, two-party politics has given way to a three-party system, with the Liberal Democrats challenging the long domination of the Conservative and Labour parties. Furthermore, as the Republican party's displacement of the Whigs during the 1854–1860 period demonstrates, a new party can overcome structural barriers by changing the nation's agenda. It is, of course, fortunate for the United States— though unfortunate for third parties—that no issue as divisive as slavery has restructured American politics since the 1850s.

Assessing Public Support for the Republicans and Democrats

Public opinion polls have revealed considerable discontent with the existing political order and a willingness to accept an alternative party on the ballot. These data are significant indicators of public unease with the political system but should not blind one to the extent of voter support for the Republican and Democratic parties—support that a third party would have to overcome in order to be viable on a continuing basis.

Approximately two-thirds of voters in the electorate identify themselves as either Democrats or Republicans. It is true that party loyalty has declined in recent decades, yet the degree of loyalty **party identifiers** show for their party is impressive. Thus, in the four presidential elections between 1980 and 1992, 90 percent of strong Democrats voted for the Democratic nominee; weak Democrats did so on average 67 percent of the time. Republican identifiers showed even higher levels of party loyalty (strong Republicans 93 percent, weak Republicans 81 percent; see Smith et al., 1995:10). These patterns of party loyalty continued through the 2000 election. Exit polls showed that 91 percent of Republican identifiers voted for George W. Bush, whereas 86 percent of Democrats supported Al Gore. Even 67 percent of self-identified liberal Republicans and 88 percent of moderate Republicans were supportive of their party's nominee; 73 percent of conservative Democrats and 86 percent of moderate Democrats voted for Gore.

Perhaps an even stronger indicator of the major parties' support within the electorate is the fact that those who claim to be independents, but "lean" toward one of the major parties, demonstrate remarkably high levels of major party preference inside the voting booth. For the period 1980–1992, 71 percent of "**Democratic leaners**" on average voted for the Democratic presidential nominee, and 79 percent of "**Republican leaners**" voted Republican (Smith et al., 1995:10; see also Keith et al., 1992). According to the 2000 National Election Study, independents who lean either way continued to show high levels of party loyalty. Democratic-leaning independents voted 72 percent for Gore; Republican-leaning independents voted 79 percent for George W. Bush. True independents split evenly, with both Gore and Bush gaining 43.5 percent of their votes. It would thus appear that most independents—a potential base for a third party—are in fact closet Democrats or Republicans whose partisanship approximates that of people who openly identify with one of the major parties.

In addition to these indicators of public support for the two major parties, derived from voting behavior, a careful examination of recent public opinion data reveals that voters are actually more favorably disposed toward the existing party system than is commonly supposed. A 1995 Gallup Poll thus found that only 12 percent of respondents felt that a new party should *replace* one of the major parties (6 percent said it should replace the Republicans, and 6 percent wanted the Democrats to be replaced). The Gallup organization also found in polls conducted after the 1996 national conventions that 89 percent of the public were favorable to at least one of the major parties, whereas only 11 percent were unfavorable, neutral, or unsure about both parties. These data suggest that if the core constituency for a third party is voters who are at least neutral about the two existing parties or downright hostile toward them, then it would appear that only one voter in ten met this criterion in 1996 (Moore, 1996:13). A core constituency of this size would constitute a small base upon which to build a party capable of competing with the Republicans and Democrats.

Similarly, survey data do not offer much encouragement for a new party of the left. Among voters asked in 1994 how well each party represented "people like yourself," 32 percent gave high marks to both parties; 21 percent did so for the Republicans, 22 percent the Democrats. Of the remaining 25 percent who were not satisfied with either major party, only 5 percent identified themselves as being liberal or very liberal.

Research by Abramson et al. on Wallace (1968), Anderson (1980), and Perot (1992 and 1996) voters reveals no upheaval in the electorate's attitudes toward the major parties. Independent and third-party candidates are able to arouse attitudes that are hostile to the major parties, but those attitudes in isolation do not provide a strong enough impetus to support independent or third-party movements capable of challenging the Republican-Democratic dominance. People supporting an independent or third-party candidate "are not those harboring long-developed disaffection for the major parties, but rather are those who can be moved to express anti-party views because, and probably only because, they are disaffected from the parties' candidates, in a particular election." Thus, support for Perot was tied almost entirely to transient dissatisfaction with the major parties (Abramson et al., 2000:512).

Therefore, it appears that support for the major parties has not eroded sufficiently to provide a systemic opportunity for an independent candidate or new party to end the Republican-Democratic duopoly.

Fear of "Wasting" One's Vote: Strategic Voting in Recent Presidential Elections

With so many obstacles facing third-party and independent candidates, it would hardly be surprising if voters concluded that such a candidate had no realistic hope of being elected. Given that a vote for such a candidate would appear to be a wasted vote, then, the reasonable voter might be expected to set aside personal preferences and cast a ballot for either the Republican or Democratic candidate—whichever was the voter's second choice. In fact, there is evidence from the 1968, 1980, and 1992 presidential elections—each of which featured significant independent or third-party candidates—that voters do engage in this type of **strategic voting**.

The extent of such strategic voting, of not "wasting" votes, is shown in Table 3.1. The most striking instance involves voters who in 1980 ranked independent John Anderson as their first choice for president. Only 57 percent of pro-Anderson voters actually cast their ballots for him; 25 percent voted for Democratic candidate

TABLE 3.1   Strategic Voting Hurts Third-Party and Independent Candidates, 1968, 1980, 1992

Year	Third Party/ Independent Candidate	Presidential Vote by Persons Whose First Choice was Third-Party or Independent Candidate (percent)		
		Democratic Candidate	Third Party/ Independent	Republican Candidate
1968	Wallace	1	84	15
1980	Anderson	25	57	18
1992	Perot	12	79	9

Source: Derived from Paul R. Abramson et al., "Third-party and Independent Candidates: Wallace, Anderson, and Perot," *Political Science Quarterly* 110 (1995): 361.

Jimmy Carter, 18 percent for Republican Ronald Reagan. The Carter campaign encouraged defections from Anderson because it rightfully feared that his candidacy would take more votes from Carter than from Reagan.

Ross Perot's presidential bid was also hurt in a significant way by the 21 percent of supporters who ultimately decided to vote for a major party candidate. There were small-scale defections to Republican and Democratic candidates (16 percent) among pro–George Wallace voters in 1968. Clearly, fear of wasting one's vote is a significant barrier facing third parties and independent candidates (Abramson et al., 1995). Interestingly, this is true even when the candidate has the financial resources, as Perot did in 1992, to fund a competitive campaign.

This tendency toward strategic voting was also seen in 2000. More than 90 percent of those who rated either Buchanan or Nader as their preferred candidate voted for someone else. Among those who preferred Nader, 53.0 percent cast ballots for Gore, 37.6 percent voted for Bush, 48.1 percent abstained, and only 9.4 percent voted for Nader. Among those who preferred Buchanan, Bush got 46.3 percent; Gore received 43.9 percent; a mere 3.5 percent cast their votes for Buchanan, and 39.8 percent abstained (Burden, 2001:4).

Multiparty Systems at the State Level: The Overwhelming Tides of National Politics

State politics has seen several examples of multiparty systems in which third parties competed effectively with the Republicans and Democrats. In spite of institutional arrangements that inhibit third parties, viable third parties were temporarily successful in Minnesota and Wisconsin during the 1930s and early 1940s, winning governorships, controlling legislative chambers, and electing U.S. senators and representatives. The Minnesota Farmer-Labor party and the Progressives of Wisconsin led by the La Follettes temporarily displaced the Democrats as one of the major parties in state politics. As impressive as these third-party successes were in the otherwise nearly universal domination of the Republicans and Democrats, their short duration as flourishing parties is of much greater significance (Epstein, 1986:125).

These multiparty systems at the state level collapsed in the 1940s and stand as testimony to the difficulties third parties face when operating within an electoral system in which voters align themselves in national politics between two major parties and then are required to align themselves among three parties in state elections. The Minnesota and Wisconsin third parties died as distinct entities in the 1940s and were forced to merge into the major parties because the tides of national politics overwhelmed them. With party attachments being forged in the fires of national politics, it became impossible for these parties to maintain their separate identities and retain a reasonable chance of winning elections. Political scientist Leon D. Epstein has described the disintegration of Wisconsin's Progressive party and the three-party system it fostered in the 1930s and 1940s:

> When the Republicans were again effectively challenged after World War II, it was by the new state Democratic party whose leaders were very much in line with the northern liberalism of the national party, specifically with its presidential campaigns. The third-party Progressives had not been able to retain the loyalty of voters, who now, particularly in urban areas, identified with the Democratic party of FDR [Franklin D. Roosevelt] and Truman in national politics. The national electoral alignment was simply too strong a force to counter, and Wisconsin reemerged as an arena for competition between Republicans and Democrats. (Epstein, 1986:126)

In recent years, third parties at the state level have formed around prominent and colorful leaders who once were officeholders of the Republican party. Thus, in 1990 former U.S. Senator Lowell Weicker led his own party in Connecticut to a gubernatorial election victory, and former governor Walter Hickel, running on the Alaska Independent party label, reclaimed the governorship. However, both of these state-level experiments in third-party politics withered after their leaders ceased to head the ticket. The group called A Connecticut Party (ACP) received only 19 percent of the vote for governor in 1994 without Weicker as its candidate, and the Alaskan Independence party, without Hickel, received just 13 percent of the vote in the succeeding election.

As noted in Chapter 2, in 1998 Minnesota governor Jesse Ventura became the first Reform party candidate to win major statewide office. However, in 2000 the capture of the party's national nominating convention by the right-wing forces of Pat Buchanan caused Ventura to leave the party. He retained his popularity with Minnesota voters, but his Independence party, which he formed for the 2000 elections, was not effective in competing with the major parties in congressional and state legislative elections.

Although the tides of national politics have overwhelmed the midwestern states that once embraced third parties, as well as states that have recently seen leaders seek a "third way" to govern, recent research has revealed that some western states have the ingredients for multiparty politics. In these states, partisan cleavages within the electorate created by national and state politics are out of alignment, thereby creating an opening for third parties. However, even in these states, the prospects for third parties are dim because institutional arrangements like the direct primary and single-member districts "push would-be third party voters to a choice of two candidates for office running under national party labels" (Gimpel, 1996:207; see also Chapter 2).

An Environment Hostile to Third Parties

The cultural and institutional environments in America are not conducive to developing and sustaining a thriving multiparty system. Support for the major parties remains relatively stable, with even independent "leaners" showing remarkable levels of party loyalty. Institutional arrangements impose major barriers to third parties and bolster the electoral dominance of the Republicans and the Democrats. These institutional barriers are not likely to be changed in the foreseeable future because the most imposing of these barriers are deeply imbedded in the political system and enjoy widespread popular support. This support is particularly true for the direct primary system, presidential primaries, single-member legislative districts, and separation of powers. The Electoral College, the Federal Election Campaign Act, and state ballot access laws, which help perpetuate the status quo, do not command comparable public support, but neither do they generate the public interest or displeasure required for major changes that could benefit third parties. The prospects for institutional reforms that could aid third parties are therefore bleak.

In examining the role and prospects for third parties in the United States, it is also necessary to examine how third parties, minor parties, and independent candidates are actually operating in America's unfriendly environment. Recent and current third-party activities, strategies, and impacts are the focus of Chapter 4, in which we also examine the response of the major parties to would-be challengers.

Ultimately, the supreme test of any party system in a democracy is whether it contributes to citizens' control of their governmental leaders, maintenance of political stability, and relatively effective policymaking. How well the American party system serves the American people will be the concern of Chapter 5.

4

···

The Public Demand
for Alternatives

H. Ross Perot (right) announced his presidential candidacy in 1992 on CNN's
Larry King Live show.

Up to this point, we have shown that the nation has a long history of two-party politics and that legal and institutional structures support that electoral system. With such a rich history, how much credence should be given to the detractors of two-party politics in the United States? What evidence of dissatisfaction exists? What is the true scope of the two-party system dilemma in the contemporary context?

In this chapter, we lay out the evidence that discontent with the current system exists, and we attempt to specify the causes of dissatisfaction. Our evidence will come mainly from national politics, but we will look at the experiences of states as well. Finally, we examine the consequences of the various ways in which the two-party system has been challenged in recent years. In evaluating those experiments with our electoral systems, we will anticipate the normative argument presented in the concluding chapter.

Discontent at the Ballot Box with Two-Party Alternatives

Although we have stated that Americans have continuously expressed dissatisfaction with two-party politics and expressed an appropriate caveat about the extent of that discontent, it is clear that the level of dissatisfaction in the last decade was unusually high. Look at the evidence from the five elections in the 1990s.

In 1990, citizens in two states, Alaska and Connecticut, chose third-party candidates to be their governors. Both Walter Hickel in Alaska and Lowell Weicker in Connecticut rejected the politics of the two major parties. They each had statewide reputations and had been elected previously as Republicans. But in 1990 their appeal was based on presenting alternatives different from those of the two major parties.

In 1992, of course, Ross Perot polled more votes as an independent candidate for president than had any third-party candidate since former president Theodore Roosevelt rejected the policies of his successors in the Republican party and ran on the Bull Moose ticket in 1912. In some ways the most impressive aspect of Perot's showing was the extent to which it was based more on rejection of what the major parties were offering than on a positive alternative of his own.

Oversimplifying slightly, one could argue that Perot's appeal went something like this: "These politicians aren't getting the job done. They are only concerned with serving their own interests, not 'ours.' I've got an incredible record of success. Reject them and give me a chance to fix the mess they've gotten us into." He hit a responsive chord; late into the campaign, polls showed him leading the two major party candidates. The level of support he maintained caused traditional party politicians to stand up and take notice. Few decisions were made in the immediate aftermath of the 1992 election without considering their impact on Perot and his supporters.

The 1992 congressional election was marked by the defeat of twenty-four incumbents and by the near defeat of many more. Although only Bernie Sanders of Vermont was elected without major party backing, a record number of parties filed candidates to run for Congress (Collet, 1996b), and the electorate appeared to be rejecting politics-as-usual.

That trend was continued in the 1994 congressional election, in which the Republicans captured control of the House of Representatives for the first time in forty years and recaptured control of the Senate, which they had lost at the end of the Reagan administration. No Republican representative elected to the 104th Congress had ever served in the majority in the House; on the Democratic side, fewer than five had ever served in the minority. The 1994 election has been interpreted in many ways (see, e.g., the articles in Klinckner, 1996), but it is difficult not to see it as a rejection of politics-as-usual. In 1992, Bill Clinton had campaigned as a New Democrat, willing to reject old, failed approaches and to adopt a more pragmatic approach to problem-solving. During his first two years in office, he governed as an Old Democrat, ceding power to the same interests that had dominated his party for years. The voters rejected that approach and chose instead the Republicans' Contract with America.

But the first reactions to Republican attempts to implement the Contract with America during the 104th Congress were highly negative. Newt Gingrich of Georgia, the architect of the Republican victory and the leading spokesperson for the agenda embedded in the Contract, assumed and was granted vast powers at the beginning of his term as Speaker of the House. As the public became aware of the details behind the rhetoric, however, Gingrich's popularity plummeted. Halfway through the first Congress they had controlled in four decades, the Republicans and their solutions to the nation's ills were no more popular than the Democrats they had replaced.

In the 1994 election, Angus King of Maine followed the lead set by Hickel and Weicker four years earlier. A successful entrepreneur and businessman, King had been active in Democratic party politics earlier in his career. He was well known throughout the state as the longtime host of a TV talk show examining state government, and he invested part of his personal fortune in his own campaign. That campaign took advantage of statewide dissatisfaction with partisan battles and ethical scandals; King decried government inefficiency and claimed he would get government out of the way so that Maine's economy could move forward. His successful campaign was a natural in a state with a long tradition of supporting third-party candidates.[1]

King was not the only non-major party gubernatorial candidate to do well in 1994. In Hawaii, Frank Fasi, who was mayor of Honolulu from 1968 to 1980 and again from 1984 until the 1994 election, finished second behind Democrat Ben Cayetano, ahead of former congresswoman Pat Saiki, the Republican candidate. Fasi formed his own party, the Best party, trying to draw on dissatisfaction with the major parties. His appeal, not unlike Perot's, was that he had a record of accomplishment that the citizens could trust. Although he did not win, he drew nearly one-third of the votes cast.[2]

In eight of the other thirty-four states holding gubernatorial elections in 1994, one or more non-major party candidates polled at least 5 percent of the vote. In seven of those races, the votes they attracted were enough to deny the victor a majority—or perhaps to alter the outcome of the election. Many more states hold statewide elections in nonpresidential election years than in years in which presidents are chosen; thus, the 1994 election is good evidence that the two major parties no longer have total dominance over politics in a number of states.[3]

In the 1996 election, President Clinton became the first Democrat since Franklin Delano Roosevelt to win reelection; but the election did not signal a return to old patterns. The Republicans retained control of both houses of Congress, despite the poor showing of their presidential candidate (Bob Dole) and the unpopularity of their most visible legislative leader, Speaker Gingrich. Although Ross Perot polled fewer than half as many votes as in 1992, his showing was significant for a number of reasons. First, the Reform party, *as a party*, qualified for the ballot in all fifty states. Second, even though Perot disappointed his followers, the Reform party's share of the vote qualified its candidate for federal funding in the 2000 election and made Perot the first non-major party candidate in this century—in fact since the Republican party came into existence—to win more than 5 percent of the vote in two consecutive elections. Third, the Reform party ran candidates for a number of offices below the presidential level and began to develop the organizational infrastructure necessary to maintain itself into the future.

In the 1998 election, incumbents were reelected to the U.S. Congress in traditionally high numbers; only one of those incumbents was not a Democrat or a Republican. But two states elected governors from a party other than the major parties, with the reelection of King in Maine and the election of Ventura in Minnesota. Following the trend observed earlier, we note that third-party candidates ran for governor in thirty-six states, and eight of those received more than 5 percent of the vote.

Another development from recent elections has been the emergence and growth of so-called new parties. In 1994, for example, the Libertarian party ran fifteen candidates for governor, another fifteen for the U.S. Senate, and eighty-one for the U.S. House of Representatives. In 1996, it ran 126 candidates for House or Senate; in 1998, 173 candidates; and in 2000, 266 candidates. It continued to run candidates for governor in most of the states in which it was active. The Green party does not have a history as long as that of the Libertarians in this country, but the Greens have also expanded their efforts below the presidential level. In 1994, the Green party ran six candidates for House or Senate; one of the House candidates polled enough votes that likely would have gone to the Democrat to give the victory to the Republican. In 1996 and 1998, Greens only ran seven candidates; but in 2000, reflecting their effort to build into a true alternative party, they fielded forty-five candidates for House and Senate seats throughout the nation.

We note the development of these new parties because what is happening in the United States has clear parallels in other democracies. Although we have focused on third parties that have had short-term electoral significance, the long history of political battles between Democrats and Republicans in the United States and the not-inconsequential obstacles to third-party development noted in Chapter 3 do not mean that victory by the two major parties in this country or even the continued existence of those two parties is inevitable. We do not believe that these new parties will have a history different from traditional minor parties, but because their appeal is different, that possibility does exist.

Ask the Progressive Conservative party in Canada. In the 1984 parliamentary elections in Canada, the Progressive Conservatives, or Tories, wrested control from the Liberals, winning 211 seats. They maintained their control for nine years, through the prime ministerships of Brian Mulroney and Kim Campbell. Then came the 1993 elections. The Tories suffered a crushing defeat, going from the majority party with 154 seats to holding only two seats and losing official party status (Farnsworth, 1993). The Liberal party, led by Jean Chrétien, swept the Progressive Conservatives out of office, acquiring 177 seats.

In June 1997, Chrétien called for an election, hoping to solidify the Liberal party's power. But that election did not produce the expected results, either. The Liberals received only 38 percent of the national vote and a razor-thin parliamentary majority. The opposition was split, with the Reform party dominant in the western provinces of British Columbia, Alberta, and Saskatchewan. The New Democrats made their strongest showing in the Prairie and Atlantic provinces but were not dominant in either. The Progressive Conservatives won a majority of the seats in the Maritime provinces of Nova Scotia and New Brunswick. Bloc Quebecois carried the province of Quebec. The Reform party captured a total of sixty seats, gaining the title of official opposition. In the election held in October 2000, Chrétien and his party were reelected, with a slightly larger parliamentary majority, but still polling only about 40 percent of the vote. Ten other parties fielded candidates for Parliament. The Progressive Conservatives finished fifth, with only twelve seats in the legislature; again the Canadian Reform Conservative Alliance placed second, retaining their status as the official opposition.

Do you think the Tories in Great Britain, looking at the results of their 1997 defeat, did not fear the Canadian comparison? They had gained control of the legislature in 1979 and dominated British government for a full eighteen years, much of it under the leadership of Prime Minister Margaret Thatcher. The 1997 election, however, marked the worst performance by the Conservatives in nearly a century, with Labour gaining an overwhelming majority. Furthermore, the Liberal Democrats managed to double their standing in the House of Commons (Hames, 1997). Only a massive victory, such as in 1924 when the Tories won 223 seats, ousting Labour, would be sufficient to remove Tony Blair from power. In the 2002 British election, the Tories made only slim inroads on Blair's majority; the Liberal Democrats did not make gains as dramatic as they had three years earlier, but again they improved their standing and closed the gap between them and the Tories. How secure can politicians anywhere be when they look at these examples—or at other democracies such as Japan, where the Liberal Democrats had held power for thirty-seven years prior to their loss in 1993, then were able to reverse that verdict four years later? What once seemed predictable might be much less so in the current electoral environment.

One can look at American political history since the formation of the Republican party in 1854 and see a stable two-party system unlikely to be disturbed. That would be the picture that Chapter 2 would lead you to expect. Or one can look at American electoral results from the 1990s and at recent historic changes in the similarly stable political systems of our economic allies and see evidence of societies in flux and political systems strained by that fluidity. It is in this context that we ask whether the dissatisfaction with our two-party system in evidence today is different from the normal background-noise-level expressions of discontent.

Public Opinion on the Performance of Our Two-Party Political System

In a most useful compilation appearing in *Public Opinion Quarterly*, Christian Collet (1996a) has summarized three decades of public opinion polling, conducted in a variety of national surveys, on various aspects of how Americans see their political system.[4] At the most general level, in a *Los Angeles Times* poll taken in October of 1995, nearly one-half of the respondents answered that they thought the two-party system in this country was basically unsound (49 percent of 1,426 polled).

The more important questions involve alternatives to the two-party system, particularly investigating how citizens view those alternatives compared to how they did at earlier periods. This information is somewhat difficult to obtain because polling organizations have changed the ways questions are worded over a period of time, but some indications are clear.

If we search earlier polls, for example, the Roper and Gallup organizations have asked questions about satisfaction with the two-party system or desire for different kinds of alternatives over a period of years. In a May 1938 Roper poll (of 5,151 respondents), 65 percent said they favored the current system, whereas only 13 percent wanted a strong third party added to the Republicans and Democrats, and 6 percent said they wanted two new parties on a liberal-conservative spectrum. In another Roper poll, this one in May 1944 (5,131 respondents), 78 percent said that they were usually satisfied with the stands taken by the two major parties, whereas only 14 percent said they would like to see a new party. Answering a variation of the same question in September 1968, 67 percent of Gallup's respondents (n=1,500) were satisfied with the choice between the two major parties; 27 percent favored a third party with principles more in line with their points of view.

Contemporary respondents give a very different set of answers. In a September 1995 CNN/*USA Today* poll (640 respondents), 53 percent wanted a new third party to exist along with the Democratic and Republican parties, 12 percent wanted a new party to replace one or both of the existing major parties, and only 26 percent wanted the system to continue as it is. In a series of polls conducted for the Times-Mirror Center for the People and the Press by Princeton Survey Research Associates, in July 1994 (n=3,800), April 1995 (n=1,800), and October 1995 (n=2,000), 53 percent, 57 percent, and 59 percent, respectively, agreed with the view that the nation should have a third party in addition to the major parties. In polls taken in November (n=744) and December (n=1,111) 1995 and in April 1996 (n=1,257), approximately the same percentages (51 percent, 57 percent, and 53 percent, respectively) agreed with a CBS News/*New York Times* survey suggestion that the country needs a new political party to compete with the two major parties in offering the best candidate for political office. In poll after poll taken by these organizations, as well as in those conducted by ABC News/*Washington Post* and *Time*/CNN during the same period, nearly three out of every five respondents said they favor having a third-party alternative discussing issues and presenting candidates for offices, in opposition to the Republicans and the Democrats (Collet, 1996a:444).

Interestingly, the public seems somewhat unclear about what kind of alternative is desirable. In July 1992 in a Louis Harris and Associates poll (n=1,256 respondents), 29 percent said they wanted a "continuation of the two-party system of Democrats and Republicans," and 30 percent favored the growth of one or more new parties to challenge the two existing major parties, but 38 percent wanted elections in which individuals ran without party label. When a similar question was asked by the National Election Study in 1994 (n=1,774 respondents), 37 percent favored candidates running without party label.

These results indicate a lack of faith in the parties as well as the desire for different alternatives. Calls for a new third party or support for third-party candidates are often confused with a desire for independence from party politics altogether. These responses equate to different, though equally serious, threats to the two-party system.

In October 1994 (n=1,509) and again in September 1995 (n=1,005), an NBC News/*Wall Street Journal* poll asked citizens how likely they would be to support an unspecified third-party candidate. Forty-three percent in 1994 and 49 percent in 1995 answered that the likelihood of their supporting a third-party candidate was 50-50 or better. A CNN/*USA Today* poll in September 1995 (n=640) found that 43 percent thought it was "not too important" or "not at all important" for the president to be from one of the two major parties.

Finally, one can look at polling data on specific third-party candidates for president. In the 1980 presidential campaign, John Anderson's polling numbers peaked at about 24 percent in a Gallup Poll conducted in mid-June. In May 1992, 39 percent claimed that they favored Ross Perot over George Bush and Bill Clinton. Virtually every polling organization found support for General Colin Powell to be in the middle to upper 30 percent range in late 1995 (in a four-way race with Clinton, Dole, and Perot, who was also receiving around 10 percent, depending on the specific poll examined), when his candidacy was under most serious consideration. Although actual support for third-party candidates has tended to wane as election day approached and as voters have been besieged by the major parties with appeals not to waste their votes (see Chapter 3), these early indications of support demonstrate a public willingness to look for alternatives.

These polling data tell us that the dilemma we have identified is real and of a different level of intensity than at other periods in recent American political history. American voters are dissatisfied with the two-party system as it functions today; they are dissatisfied with the choices that have been presented to them; they are willing to look for alternatives and to consider supporting those who present themselves.

Even so, what is disliked by the public is clearer than what is desired. Saying that a certain percentage of the populace would like an alternative to consider is not the same as saying that voters would all like the same alternative to consider. As we demonstrated earlier, the public is presented today, and has been presented before, with alternatives. Candidates with visibility and credibility have run against the major party candidates for president in 1948 (Strom Thurmond and Henry Wallace), 1968 (George Wallace), 1980 (John Anderson), 1992 and 1996 (Ross Perot), and 2000 (Ralph Nader and Pat Buchanan). Minor party candidates, representing either traditional doctrinaire minor parties or new, culturally based minor parties, have appeared on the ballot for president and for many other offices. A few of these candidates have won statewide or local offices, and others have received considerable support in losing efforts, but none has created a political organization to answer the public's call for the type of alternative people seem to desire.

One would think that politicians, always eager to please the public in order to achieve victory, would heed the call for alternatives. We turn next to examining their response.

Politicians' Responses to Public Discontent

Politicians have responded to the public discontent noted here in a number of different ways. The key to the issue relates to which politicians one is interested in observing.

Consider first those politicians who are challenged by a serious and visible third-party opponent. We have prominent examples in recent elections—George Bush and Clinton facing Perot in 1992; Clinton and Dole facing Perot again in 1996; Gore and George W. Bush facing Nader in 2000; U.S. Representatives John Rowland (R) and Bruce Morrison (D), who finished second and third, respectively, to Weicker in Connecticut; former Anchorage mayor Tony Knowles (D) and state senator Arlis Sturgulweski (R), who trailed Hickel; in Hawaii, Ben Cayetano (D), who beat Frank Fasi, and former U.S. representative Pat Saiki (R), who lost to Fasi; former governor and congressman Joseph Brennan (D) and Senate staffer Susan Collins (R), who lost to King in Maine; longtime elected officials and party leaders Skip Humphrey (D) and Norm Coleman (R), who lost to Ventura in 1998. A number of themes are clear.

Although they would not say so publicly, all of these major party candidates wished that the third-party contender would go away. Put simply, it is easier to campaign against a known quantity—an adversary who is running under a label and whose appeal is quite predictable—than it is to plot a strategy when the impact of an entrant into the race is unknown. Minor party candidates on the ballot can be an irritant; but serious contenders have made necessary the rethinking of basic strategy with too many unknowns. No major party candidate can be happy undertaking an enterprise as important and complex as a statewide or national campaign without having a good idea of what needs to be done to maximize votes. Politics is at best an art and not a science. With two parties in the race, the art is intelligible; with three contenders, it becomes more abstract.

Of course, major party candidates cannot force serious third-party or independent contenders off the ballot. And that is precisely the problem they face: an entrant over whom they have no control. Thus, they must react to a new situation. In virtually all cases, reactions are based on strategic considerations, not philosophical views.

A number of strategic choices occur. First, the established party politicians have to decide how serious a contender any entrant is. When a candidate is a former governor or senator, as Hickel and Weicker were, or when entrants announce their willingness to spend significant amounts of their own money to get their message out, as Perot (in 1992) and King each did, or when the third-party contender has a proven track record, as Perot did in 1996, then all major party candidate decisions must take the minor party candidate into account. In other cases, major party candidates can try to ignore alternative candidates—but always with a great deal of risk.

This risk was never clearer than in the 2000 presidential race. Vice President Al Gore had to make a decision about the seriousness of the Nader challenge to his Democratic base. In diverting resources to counter Nader's influence in some states, such as Oregon, he might well have not put enough emphasis on other states, such as New Hampshire. However, other strategic decisions might have had equally unfavorable results.

The next judgment deals with whether the third-party candidate will hurt your candidacy more than your opponent's, if that can be estimated. Polling data on third-party nominees is notoriously unreliable; strategists rely on whatever hard data they can obtain, but much more on instinct. Frequently, the best guess is that the "intruder" will hurt one candidate more in some geographic sections or more with some subsets of the population and less in others. The Republican and Democratic candidates have to walk a tightrope, trying to reclaim their own party supporters without alienating those whose leanings are uncertain. In three of the four state races cited, one major party candidate trailed badly—the Democrat in Connecticut and the Republican in the races in Alaska and Maine. In that situation, the candidate who runs third must try to find a way to save face. The contending major party candidate has to decide whether to cement his or her own base or to appeal across party lines to defeat the real threat—the third-party candidate. It is difficult to make these judgments when so much of the information on which strategists must rely is "soft" at best. In the Minnesota example, the entire race was close, and the rush to Ventura at the end of the campaign was unexpected. Again, strategic judgments were difficult to make.

The balancing act involves deciding how to respond to the third-party candidate's stand on salient issues, how to deal with inclusion or exclusion of that candidate from any proposed debates, whether to assert at the end of the campaign that a vote for that candidate is a wasted vote—because only one of the two major party candidates can really win—or whether to appear magnanimous by treating the third candidate as an equal.

Political campaigns are about winning and losing, not about debating the electoral system. In the 1992 presidential campaign, candidates Bush and Clinton had no choice but to accept Ross Perot as a legitimate contender. Early poll results showed that he was being taken seriously by the public. The Commission on Presidential Debates included him in televised debates. The media treated him as a candidate who would have an impact on the election's result even if he did not win. He was spending tens of millions of dollars to get his message across. The only choices Bush and Clinton really had involved setting strategy in answering this threat, as Perot was in fact leading both of them in the polls between the time they each secured their nominations by winning enough delegate support and were officially designated as nominees at their parties' national conventions. The problem for President Bush was especially vexing, as Perot's campaign stresses criticism of the Republican party and particularly President Bush's handling of the economy.

Between the 1992 and 1996 elections, both major parties made explicit appeals to the Perot supporters. In fact, ten of the major contenders for the Republican nomination and a coterie of White House strategists made pilgrimages to a United We Stand organizational conference in Dallas in August 1995, in attempts to show that they viewed the opinions of these citizens as worthy of note, and in hope of obtaining a Perot endorsement and fending off a 1996 Perot-sponsored campaign.

When Perot decided to enter the campaign in 1996, President Clinton's strategists took a very different tack from those of Republican nominee Bob Dole. Clinton had a solid lead and felt that most of the Perot support was coming from voters who otherwise might support former Senator Dole. Thus, he could appear magnanimous and claim that he thought Perot should be included in televised debates. But he did not want to be too generous. He therefore stated that he thought Perot should be in, but he would debate without him because the American public deserved to hear the two major candidates. Dole opposed Perot's entrance into the debates—because he felt that any increase in Perot support would come at his expense—and seemed a poor sport. In fact, of course, both candidates were adopting positions that they felt helped their chances of winning.

The same strategy continued throughout the campaign. Clinton was able to ignore the Perot issue; Dole had to worry that Perot voters were those who were deserting his candidacy. Neither position had anything to do with the candidates' views on third parties; they had everything to do with how this particular third party impacted on this particular campaign (Just, 1997).

In 2000, the Gore campaign faced a somewhat different situation. The entire race was very close. The Nader appeal was not a major threat in many states, but in a few pivotal states the Green party candidate was very much a factor. The Gore strategists would like to have ignored Nader altogether, but they felt that could have disastrous results in particular areas. Thus, they did not want him to appear in the debates—such an appearance would have added to Nader's credibility nationally—but they had to confront him in particular areas. Critics claim they never found the right strategy and that Nader did in fact cost Gore the election by siphoning enough votes away to swing critical states to Bush. Others believe that the tightrope was too narrow to navigate, that no winning strategy could have been devised. But in any recounting of the 2000 election, the strategic response to the Nader candidacy from the Gore campaign must play an important role.

The same themes can be seen in statewide campaigns. In three of the four cases we have mentioned earlier in this book, Hickel, Weicker, and King were so obviously strong contenders that they could not be ignored. Hickel and Weicker were each obviously drawing support from those who had voted for them in the past. The Republican contenders had to figure out a way to keep their party loyalists in the fold; neither succeeded.[5]

In Maine, the sources of King's support were less clear. He had been a Democrat but campaigned as a businessman who could get the state's economy moving again. Strategic considerations were complicated because all concerned were acutely aware of the strength of Perot's support in the state in 1992, when he had finished ahead of President Bush, and because of the presence of another party on the ballot, the Green party. In the last month, polls showed that Republican nominee Susan Collins was trailing badly behind both King and the Democrat, former governor and congressman Joseph Brennan. Collins struggled to retain her base and to remain respectable. Brennan tried to hold Democrats, not to lose the environmental vote to King or the women's vote to Collins, and hoped that Collins would retain enough Republicans so that King did not prevail. In the end, he could not reach that balance, and King beat him by 7,878 votes (about 1 percent). Postelection analyses concluded that the Greens as well as Collins's weakness doomed the Democrat's strategy.[6]

The case of Ventura's victory is somewhat different. Ventura was considered an irritant more than a serious candidate for much of the 1998 campaign. However, he proved quite adept at gaining media attention, and the two major party candidates were not successful in persuading the electorate that they could provide new blood for state government. They were the essence of establishment politicians; Ventura was anything but. At first Ventura was denied equal treatment under the state's campaign financing laws, and he had difficulty raising money. However, as he hung around longer and longer and came to be viewed as a more serious candidate, that situation was reversed. In the closing days of the campaign he received a boost when he was declared eligible for state funding. At the same time, the two major candidates did not have the resources remaining to counter his late offensive. In point of fact, Ventura gained because he was not taken seriously for so long, and there was too little time to respond once the impact of his candidacy became clear.

Politicians running for other offices must also consider how to respond to significant third-party candidates at the top of their state's election ballots. Remember that these politicians are on the ballot because they have won either the Republican or Democratic party nomination. Most of their supporters are members of their political party—or at least that has always been the conventional wisdom. But the presence of a third-party alternative at the top of the ticket changes their strategic calculus.

At the very least, these politicians have to determine where the third-party candidate is garnering support. If the support is from their party, these politicians need to consider whether their own supporters might desert them in their race if they do oppose the minor party candidate elsewhere on the ballot too vociferously. How much has their appeal been weakened by their relationship with their own party's nominee at the top of the ballot? Do that candidate's supporters help them or not? How will they react to a lukewarm effort? To a strategic separation? Or to an outright endorsement of the third-party alternative?

The difficulty in making these judgments is compounded by lack of information. In fact, the answer to most of the questions just posed is the same: It is hard to know. Thus, politicians must rely on gut instinct. The question often comes down to a decision about which candidate—their own party's nominee or the third-party alternative—they themselves feel closer to.

Of course, these decisions depend heavily on political context. In the case of Perot's two campaigns for the presidency, many local politicians, particularly those in areas in which Perot showed early strength, shied away from their own preferred nominees. Few gave Perot outright endorsements, but a great many let their supporters know that Perot's message resonated with them as well. One not very subtle way of doing this was to echo Perot's criticisms of the way those in government were performing; not surprisingly, this course of action was more open to challengers and those running in open seats than it was to incumbents. In 1992 and 1996, observers saw many state and local candidates—Democrats in the South and doctrinaire conservative Republicans in a variety of geographic locations—stay away from the candidates at the top of their tickets, in hopes of attracting the same voters to whom Perot was appealing.

Again, the same situation occurred in those states in which strong third-party candidates appeared in 1990 and 1994. A significant number of Alaska and Connecticut Republicans backed Hickel and Weicker; many others implied that they preferred the alternative to their own party's nominees without outright endorsements. Angus King's Maine campaign was given a huge boost by an endorsement from a group of mainline Democrats who were willing to state publicly that although they had supported Joe Brennan in the past, it was time for a new direction and that King signaled that direction. Endorsements of this type are critically important because of the message they send to other major party supporters: "It's okay to have the feelings you have for this guy; we're reacting just as you are, and it doesn't make you a bad [Democrat or Republican]."

In the final analysis, major party politicians must consider whether they, too, are ready to respond to public discontent and leave the major parties in order to present an alternative. That is a major step, one rarely taken by an officeholder who seems to have a bright future running under the Democratic or Republican label. Look at the difficulty Ross Perot had in finding a capable running mate in each of his two tries for the presidency. Perot had to settle for retired admiral James Stockdale in 1992. Because Stockdale clearly hurt his campaign—during the vice presidential debate, he rhetorically asked, "What am I doing here?" and no one volunteered an answer—Perot began his hunt for a 1996 running mate much earlier. None of those on his wish list—for example, Weicker, King, Penny, New York mayor Rudolph Giuliani—showed interest. He approached former Oklahoma senator David Boren and Ohio congresswoman Marcy Kaptur, and both declined. After his own pollster Gordon Black rejected an approach, he eventually settled for Pat Choate, an economist and writer who lacked any governing or political experience. His inability to attract a well-known running mate, largely because those who had political reputations thought that Perot's campaign would not benefit them, hurt Perot's credibility. Neither of his running mates seemed competent to handle the presidency should Perot be elected and the vice president be called upon to succeed him.

Consider that Weicker and Hickel were out of office and King and Ventura had never run. People change parties, some with success and some not, but few leave both parties.[7] In fact, one striking parallel among the Perot, Hickel, Weicker, King, and Ventura cases is that few other politicians in their states left to join their causes. Many thought about it, we are certain, but few made the leap. Perot, Hickel, Weicker, King, and Ventura are politicians who caught their supporters' sense of discontent and successfully drew on it. But up until this point, they have not started third-party movements (though Ventura ran under the label of one in 1998), and their success does not presage a collapse of the two-party system as we know it, largely because other politicians have not followed them. These other politicians simply do not believe that the public discontent with the major parties is sufficient to warrant their risking their own careers.

What about those who do feel that the current state of public discontent calls for a radical change in the system? Do any well-known politicians fit into this realm? What would be their strategy? Consider the activities of the so-called Gang of Seven on the eve of the 1996 election.

As the 1996 election approached, a group of quite prominent political figures met to discuss their dissatisfaction with the alternatives the public was being offered. These men felt that the Democrats and the Republicans were not addressing the important issues of the day that were most likely to impact the twenty-first century. They did not feel that Ross Perot, much of whose appeal was based on criticism of those in office and not on well-constructed alternative strategies, was the right leader for a new movement. Meeting in fall 1995, the group's members were prominent enough and respected enough to attract media attention.

Although the group did not have an official leader, its most prominent member was Democratic senator Bill Bradley from New Jersey. Bradley had come to national prominence as a former Rhodes scholar from Princeton who went on to star for the New York Knicks in the National Basketball Association. In the U.S. Senate, he was widely respected as an expert on tax policy and as one who thought deeply about the future. He was often mentioned as a politician with the potential to hold higher national office, but his somewhat plodding style, the very opposite of charisma, seemed to hold him back. In 1990, he nearly lost his reelection bid to Christine Todd Whitman, who was later elected governor of New Jersey. Chastened by this public rebuke, Bradley sought an alternative outlet for his well-developed ideas about what America needed in the future.

Bradley found a natural ally in Paul Tsongas, the former Democratic senator from Massachusetts who had run for his party's presidential nomination in 1992. Tsongas's campaign, based on the need to face tough economic questions now in order to guarantee continued prosperity into the future, struck an unexpectedly responsive chord with the primary electorate. Although Tsongas ultimately had to suspend his campaign because he could not afford to carry his message further, he became one of the leaders of the Concord Coalition, a national group whose goal was to force the federal government to get its economic house in order.

The third member of the group, like Bradley, was a retiring politician, Minnesota representative Tim Penny. Penny, again like Bradley, had made his reputation in the Congress as a member concerned with gaining control of the federal budget. With John Kasich (R-Ohio), he had proposed an alternative budget plan in 1993 that dealt with the recurring deficit. He left the Congress claiming that its members were not willing to make the difficult decisions that the economic crisis of the moment called for, but his passion for the issue remained (see Penny and Garrett, 1995; Penny and Shier, 1996).

The remaining politicians seeking an alternative to the major parties were Weicker, King, and two Coloradans—former governor Dick Lamm and former senator and presidential hopeful Gary Hart.[8] They shared the others' concern that politicians were making decisions based on the vagaries of public opinion—and more on what would play at the polls versus their concern for the future impact of their policy choices.

Three aspects about the short-lived history of the Gang of Seven are important. First, a group of respected, somewhat prominent politicians who had had electoral success within the context of two-party politics were discouraged with the system and sought to run an electoral alternative who would present a different view of how political discourse should proceed. Second, they were unsuccessful in finding a prominent (and thus possibly successful) politician to carry their banner. Their activities drew attention among political journalists. Tsongas, Lamm, and Penny presented a paper entitled "Toward Generational Equity" that criticized the handling of the national debt by the Republicans, and the group intended to produce a manifesto that would urge parties to move toward the center. Their efforts produced a great deal of talk about finding an alternative, serious candidate; but for the 1996 campaign that talk came to naught. And third, in the final chapter of this saga, Bradley returned to the Democratic party and sought the 2000 presidential nomination in an effort to deny Vice President Al Gore a prize that many thought would go to him by default.

The difference between the appearance of third-party candidates for office and the development of third parties has essentially been this: Not enough politicians are willing to jump ship to follow a new path. None of the third-party candidates have been willing to suppress their own egos enough to encourage party development. Some felt that the Reform party had this opportunity in 1996, but in the end, Perot used it as a vehicle to push his own candidacy and was not willing to make the same kind of financial investment he had in 1992 in party development. Some might well feel that the Nader effort in 2000 will lead to the growth of the

Greens as a true and lasting third-party alternative. That history—and the role that Nader might or might not play in it—has yet to be written.

Causes of the Dissatisfaction

Although we have noted public dissatisfaction with the current two-party system and have observed that some politicians have responded to that dissatisfaction in individual elections, if not in a way to challenge the current electoral system, we have not yet explored the causes of the dissatisfaction. Perhaps understanding what has caused the dissatisfaction can explain the political reactions to it.

Public dissatisfaction with the two-party system is personality-, institution-, and result-oriented. At the level of personality, with the exception of the Reagan years, Americans have not found that their leaders have deserved their admiration since the death of John Kennedy. Lyndon Johnson paled in comparison to the charismatic Kennedy. Nixon was nearly impeached and was forced to resign over Watergate. Gerald Ford was often perceived to be a bumbler. And Jimmy Carter seemed overwhelmed by the job of president. Reagan captured the hearts of the American public for his eight years in office; detractors could never understand his appeal but marveled nonetheless at its persistence. George H. W. Bush could never shake the wimp image. Bill Clinton—well, even his supporters have had to question personal decisions he has made. Although the public's opinion of George W. Bush rose dramatically after the September 11 attacks on America, during his 2000 presidential campaign many questioned whether he was serious and intelligent enough to face the challenges of the presidency. Those who have lost to these men—Hubert Humphrey, George McGovern, Michael Dukakis, Walter Mondale, Bob Dole, and Al Gore—surely did not present stronger images.[9] To be sure, these men all had distinguished careers that led to their nomination or election, but the personal images they portrayed to the public were flawed.

We cannot go through the entire panoply of elected officials throughout the nation, but our impression is that much the same would be concluded from such a review. Do you think of your governor, your senator, or your congressman as *the* leader of your community? How many of you awaken in the morning and think how fortunate you are to have these people working for you? Even if you do think you are lucky to have such strong representatives, you are probably thinking in relative terms.

We can ask why politicians have the reputations they do, whether they are flawed individuals or merely portrayed that way, but the point is that most Americans are not happy with the quality of people in public life. Look at Table 4.1; Americans do not respect their elected officials as much as many other leaders of

TABLE 4.1 The Public's View of Various Professions (in percent)

I am going to read off a number of different occupations. For each, would you tell me if you feel it is an occupation of very great prestige, considerable prestige, some prestige, or hardly any prestige at all?

			Very great prestige:		
	2001	**2000**	**1998**	**1997**	**1992**
Doctor	61	61	61	52	50
Teacher	54	53	53	49	41
Scientist	53	56	55	51	57
Minister/Clergyman	43	45	46	45	38
Military officer	40	42	34	29	32
Policeman	37	38	41	36	34
Engineer	36	32	34	32	37
Architect	28	26	26	*	*
Member of Congress	24	33	25	23	24
Athlete	22	21	20	21	18
Entertainer	20	21	19	18	17
Lawyer	18	21	23	19	25
Journalist	18	16	15	15	15
Union leader	17	16	16	14	12
Banker	16	15	18	15	17
Accountant	15	14	17	18	14
Businessman	12	15	18	16	19

* Not asked

N=1,017 adults nationwide; margin of error, ± 3.

Source: The Harris Poll. Latest: August 15–22, 2001.

society. And they blame the existing electoral system for not presenting them with choices that lead to more respected elected officials.

The second cause of the discontent is institutional. For nearly two decades, political scientists have pointed to the disturbing tendency of members of Congress to run for reelection by running against the Congress. Essentially, their claim goes something like this: "The Congress is a terrible place in which all the members are out for themselves—except me, of course. Send me back to protect you from the Congress." These campaigns have been remarkably successful if one measures success by incumbent reelection rates. As the institution of Congress—and the same can be said for other government institutions—is viewed more and more negatively by the public, more and more incumbents are reelected (Mayer and Canon, 1999).

But institution-bashing comes at a price. According to a 1995 survey of the American public by Louis Harris and Associates, only 13 percent have "a great deal of confidence in the people running" the White House; only 10 percent have such confidence in those leading the Congress. By comparison, 43 percent of Americans have confidence in military leadership and 27 percent in the leaders of major educational institutions. For our purposes, that price is also paid by the political parties. The parties are viewed as the institutions that send people to work in government and are therefore responsible for the kind of government we have. The major complaint that citizens have with the institutions of government—particularly with legislative institutions—is that they are marked by partisan bickering.

Consider the concept of **divided government**. One could argue that divided government, the situation in which one political party controls the executive branch and the other the legislative branch, is a perfect example of how separation of powers should work. Our president and our Congress are elected separately and have separate constituencies to which they are accountable. The same is true in all fifty states. This constitutional arrangement was designed to prevent any one branch of the government from becoming too powerful; it is a check against government domination of the lives of the people.

More recently, however, critics have complained that divided government has meant stagnation and the inability to get things done. That is because of the partisan nature of the negotiations among the branches of the government. Divided government is not a new phenomenon (Fiorina, 1996). David Mayhew (1991) has pointed out that divided government does not necessarily mean less-effective government. But in recent years the partisan differences have often translated into personal differences. The impression that citizens have is that the parties control the legislators and that they are more interested in their own advancement than in effective government.

Journalists have contributed to this impression as well. Complex policy differences are reduced to "the Democrats want this and the Republicans want that." Examples of effective bipartisan cooperation, such as the health care bill calling for transportability of insurance coverage that was sponsored by Republican senator Nancy Kassebaum of Kansas and Democratic senator Edward Kennedy of Massachusetts and that was passed by the Republican-controlled Congress and signed into law by the Democratic president in 1995, receive much less attention than do partisan squabbles over how a hearing will be run or whose budget numbers should be used to determine the extent to which the federal deficit has been reduced. Press stories with conflict built into them are more appealing than those praising the process. The parties are viewed as the sources of conflict. As the public tires of bickering and personal attacks, the parties are viewed as the institutional source of dissatisfaction.

Of course, the third source of discontent—lack of results—is related to the partisan conflict we have just noted. In their platforms and in making their cases to the public in election years, the two major parties make promises. Perhaps, if all of those running on one party label or the other were elected overwhelmingly, they would fulfill their promises. But election results rarely give one party or the other the opportunity to govern without considering the views of the opposition. Consequently, platform and campaign promises are not kept, and the public is disappointed.

Health care is a perfect example of this experience. In 1992, President Clinton emphasized that universal health care would be one of the top priorities of his administration. He was elected. He and the First Lady, who headed the administration's Health Care Task Force, put a good deal of effort into proposing legislation. In the end, they failed. They failed because no consensus emerged as to what kind of health care system our nation should have. Platform promises respond to public dissatisfaction. Legislation is an effort to find a workable solution to address that dissatisfaction. Recognizing a problem is easy; saying one is going to respond to it is easy. But finding a workable solution to enduring problems is difficult. Were it easy, others would have found solutions before the public's level of concern rose.

The political process builds in disappointment. Politicians want to be responsive to the needs of the people. They listen to concerns and note what their constituents want the government to do better. And they promise to fix what is wrong. But they inevitably fail—or more correctly, they usually come up with partial solutions. Solutions are partial because in a country as vast and diverse as this one—and even in states as vast and diverse as many of ours—genuine disagreement about the principles that should structure solutions to pressing problems prevent a consensus from arising. When the system works best, the result is a compromise that maximizes what people gain. When it works worst, the result is a stalemate.

Everyone in this nation, the wealthiest nation in the world, thinks that basic health care should be available to all citizens. But should health care be provided through the private sector or through a public agency? How should it be provided? What choices should citizens have? What level of health care is minimally acceptable?

Large majorities in this nation think that students should have the chance to get the education they need to build a better life, that too many children are born out of wedlock, that too many abortions are performed every year, that the nation's economy should continue to grow with little unemployment and low inflation rates, that we as a nation should be respected throughout the world, that the government should not build the federal debt endlessly, that we should be free of the threat of terrorists without surrendering our civil liberties—the list could go on and on.

It is easy to state broad societal goals in general terms. But it is difficult to determine the means to achieve them. Who should pay for higher education, and who should provide it? How intrusive should the government be in citizens' private lives? What is the government's responsibility for those who are not able to get ahead in today's society? How much of a role should the government play in managing the economy, and what trade-offs between growth and inflation are acceptable? What is the U.S. role in foreign crises—and what do we do about sovereign nations that do not share our views? What programs are cut or what taxes are raised to balance the federal budget? The answers to the "means" questions have consequences over which reasonable people differ. Thus, the problems remain unresolved—or only partial solutions are posed—and citizens become dissatisfied with the process because of unfulfilled political promises and perceived problems growing worse.

The discontent with our political parties is caused in part by unreasonable expectations that remain unfulfilled. We want our public officials to be heroes; they are mere men and women. We want our political institutions to function perfectly because we think our Constitution created a form of government that others should emulate. The Constitution was designed to make governing difficult, not easy; tension among the institutions was one of the main contributions of the founders. We want our political parties to find answers to the problems that confront our society; but it is easy to recognize problems and most difficult to craft consensual solutions in a nation as broad and diverse as ours. The Democratic and Republican parties that dominate our political landscape have become convenient whipping boys whom we punish for these unfulfilled promises, in part at least because few have any incentives to defend them.

Consequences of "Alternative" Governments

Rarely in social science are there real-world experiments that one can observe to see the impact of fundamental changes in the way society functions. However, we do have at least proximate experiments so that we can observe how our government would function with a third party in power.

At the national level, a third party has not been elected into office since the Republicans replaced the Whigs in 1860. Of course, we would not want to repeat the national trauma that followed Lincoln's election; but to be fair, the Civil War was not a consequence of Lincoln's election. The nation was divided on a fundamental issue to which the government could not respond. The depth of that division led to both the Civil War and a fundamental transformation in the party system. Similarly, because the governmental contexts are so different, we should not look to other nations' experiences to see how a third party reaching electoral prominence would impact on our system.

But, as we noted earlier, we do have three recent examples of states in which non-major party governors were elected to govern in what had previously been two-party environments. We would be remiss if we did not look, at least briefly, at the consequences of these experiments with "alternative" governments.

In Alaska, Walter Hickel was elected governor in 1990 as a candidate of the Alaskan Independence party, after failing to win gubernatorial races in 1974, 1978, and 1986 as a Republican. Hickel's party called for Alaska to secede from the union. He was elected over two candidates who had each won hotly contested primaries in their own parties. Each was an environmentalist; Hickel favored more rapid development. His one term was marked by intense controversy, including an unsuccessful attempt by his own party to recall him from office. His job rating remained low throughout his term. Hickel toyed with running for reelection in 1994, either as a Republican or as an independent, but eventually bowed out. His 1990 Democratic opponent, Tony Knowles, was the only Democrat to pick up a governor's seat for his party in the 1994 elections. It is worth noting that no Alaskan governor since 1970 has won election with a majority of the votes cast, as independents and third-party candidates have always polled quite well. The politics of Alaska have been described as those of "a state still in the making" (Barone and Ujifusa, 1994:28).

Weicker's one term as governor of Connecticut was also contentious. In 1990, he won election, under the label of A Connecticut Party (which was so named in order to fall first, alphabetically, on the ballot), when the Democrats split on the issue of an income tax and the Republican candidate stood on the same side as the winner of the Democratic primary. Weicker said that he would not rule out a tax increase and named the Democrat who had lost the primary, an income tax advocate, as his top tax adviser. Partisan bickering over the tax issue and budget matters marked Weicker's term. In a real sense, however, the issue was Weicker himself, a politician whom the *Almanac of American Politics* describes as "obstreperous, self-righteous, famously difficult to get along with; incorruptible and candid, he is also arrogant and intolerant of dissent. He is inclined to think that the only decent course to be taken is his own, and that only he is courageous enough to take it" (Barone and Ujifusa, 1994:237–238). Weicker did not seek re-election in 1994; his lieutenant governor ran on the ACP label, finishing third with 19 percent of the vote. Another independent polled 11 percent, with the result that the 1994 winner, Republican John Rowland, took office with the support of only 36 percent of the voters. Third-party politicians have left Connecticut politics in some disarray as well.

The situation in Maine has been somewhat different. Whereas Hickel and Weicker were political loners out to defeat the major parties, Angus King is an accommodator. In a state with a strong anti-major party tradition, King has shown no interest in forming a third party or in attacking the Republicans and Democrats. Rather, he has stated that he wants to work with them. The success of King's campaign grew out of public dissatisfaction with the wrangling of the two major parties that led to a shutdown of state government in 1994. King said that he wanted to "lower the volume of the debate . . . and look at the character of our leaders" (Ehrenhalt, 1991:28).

He has governed in that way since his election in 1994. Rather than fighting with major party leaders, he has tried to work with them. He has sought compromises. He has reached out to those in the legislature. But even under a collaborative approach, governing without major party backing is difficult. King has stated: "I don't have any real allies in the legislature. There is not a single person here with a stake in my success." He has likened his predicament to governing with one hand tied behind his back (Ehrenhalt, 1996:30).

Nearing the end of his second term, King remains enormously popular. The rhetorical level of political discourse in Maine has noticeably lowered. But questions remain as to whether the government can move forward without a partisan leader. According to Alan Ehrenhalt, "It is entirely possible that King will end up raising the bar for the Democrats and Republicans as well, setting standards for civility and decorum that either party will have to meet upon returning to power once the King experiment is over" (1996:31). But that is different from succeeding in presenting an alternative to the major parties. In fact, the Republicans, who fell to minority status in both houses of the state legislature after the 1996 elections, have had difficulty finding a voice to counter King or the Democrats. King won again in 1998, but in 2002 it seems likely that a major party candidate will be elected as Maine's governor. Although an independent candidate may impact the 2002 election, the Green party was divided in choosing its standard-bearer, and the Reform party seems in eclipse.

Ventura, facing reelection in 2002, is in a situation similar to that of King in 1998. He has remained popular in his state, though his ventures onto the national stage have met with mixed reviews. The success of his policies in Minnesota has been less than he would have hoped—and he has had significant conflicts with the legislature and with state employees. Yet he remains personally popular and likely to win reelection to another term.

With the exception of King's response to public discontent over the quality of individuals serving in public office and the ways in which they deal with each other, we do not conclude that the four state experiments with non-major party governance in this decade have addressed the concerns that have led to citizen discontent with the major parties. Rather, we believe that new problems have arisen and that the citizenry is legitimately just as disappointed with third-party governors as they have been with Democrats or Republicans. Moreover, we believe that effective choice and the ability to express views on the issues of the day have been obscured by the presence of these most successful third-party politicians. We turn to a normative evaluation of the dissatisfaction with two-party government in the concluding Chapter 5.

5

Political Parties in the Twenty-First Century

Minnesota governor Jesse Ventura, the only Reform party candidate to win a statewide election, with Donald Trump (left).

T̲H̲R̲E̲E̲ Q̲U̲E̲S̲T̲I̲O̲N̲S̲ R̲E̲M̲A̲I̲N̲ T̲O̲ be addressed. First, given the extent of public discontent with the Republican and Democratic parties but also recogniz ing their long history of dominating American politics, what is the likely future for the two-party system in the United States? Second, how do we evaluate the two-party system as it exists and as we see it developing in future years? Finally, what changes in the functioning of the two-party system, if any, would allow it to satisfy the needs of the polity more successfully? We turn to these questions in this final chapter.

The Future of Two-Party Politics in America

In our view, the answer to the first of these questions is that we are likely to see more of the same. The argument put forth in Chapter 3 should be recalled. The structural and institutional aspects of the American system present serious barriers to a fundamental transformation away from a two-party system.

Second place has never been very appealing to Americans; third and lower places have even less attraction. The American electoral system leads naturally to winners and losers. At the national level, the presidency is the biggest prize. One party wins. All others lose. Under our current electoral system, only two parties' candidates have an opportunity to win. All others are running symbolic campaigns.

To win the presidency, a candidate must win a *majority* of the votes in the Electoral College. If no candidate wins a majority, the House of Representatives decides the winner from among the top three finishers in electoral votes,[1] However, one must go back some time to find an election in which more than two candidates—the Democratic and the Republican candidates—won *any* electoral votes. Third-party candidates have most often been shut out because (in all states except for Nebraska and Maine) all of each state's electoral votes are awarded to the plurality winner of that state's elections, the winner-take-all system. Thus, though Ross Perot received nearly 20 percent of the national presidential vote in 1992, he received *no* electoral votes, because he was not the plurality winner anywhere.

Presidential candidates win no electoral votes for finishing a close second, much less a distant third. In fact, in the twelve presidential elections in the second half of the twentieth century, more than two candidates received electoral votes only once. The most recent example was in 1968, when American Independent party candidate George C. Wallace, the former Democratic governor of Alabama, received forty-six electoral votes, all in southern states.

Wallace's strategy is worth examining because it highlights the problems third-party candidates face in presidential politics. George Wallace built his national reputation in American politics as a defender of segregation. It was he, as governor, who stood in the door at the University of Alabama to bar the admission of the first African-American student.[2]

The Democratic party nominee in 1968 was Vice President Hubert H. Humphrey, who, as mayor of Minneapolis in 1948, had led the fight for the civil rights plank at the Democratic National Convention, a fight that caused a split in the party and led to a walkout by southern delegates, many of whom eventually backed Strom Thurmond, then the Democratic governor of South Carolina, in his States' Rights party bid for the presidency.[3] Humphrey had been a leading liberal in the Senate, particularly on social issues such as civil rights, until he was tapped as Lyndon Johnson's running mate in 1964. Humphrey was the symbol of everything Wallace opposed in the Democratic party.

However, Wallace was a savvy politician. He knew that he could not win a majority of the electoral votes in the general election. He knew he could not hope to win electoral votes in most states. But his appeal was much more regional than national. He felt that he could deny Humphrey southern votes and that those votes were more likely to go to him than to the Republican candidate, former vice president Richard Nixon. He hoped that he could win enough electoral votes, in southern states, to make it impossible for either Nixon or Humphrey to win a majority of the electoral votes.

Wallace was not naive enough to believe he could win the presidency if the election were thrown to the House of Representatives. His strategy was much more devious; he wanted to broker the Electoral College voting. When we go to the polls on election day, we are in fact voting for individual electors who in turn cast their votes for the candidate who has carried the state (see Bibby, 2000:276; Maisel, 2001, chap. 9; Best, 1996). Wallace felt that his electors would be loyal to him and would vote *in the Electoral College voting* for whomever he instructed them to support. His strategy was to negotiate with Nixon and Humphrey for policy positions and perhaps even for his own appointment as attorney general, in exchange for the support of his electors, *before the Electoral College votes were cast.*

Of course, he did not win enough electoral votes to deny Richard Nixon a majority, so this strategy was never implemented. Moreover, both Nixon and Humphrey later claimed that they would not have negotiated with Wallace, stating that his strategy undermined the electoral process. But the Wallace case is instructive because it demonstrates the lengths to which a third-party presidential candidate must go in order to have serious influence because of the winner-take-all, plurality-winner rules that govern the selection of electors in the states and the majority-winner rule that determines which candidate the Electoral College selects.

It is important to remember that the presidency is the top prize in national politics. Again, there is no credit for finishing second or third. If an election is close, we do not form coalition governments, with the loser represented in the cabinet, for example. In fact, the loser in the presidential election frequently disappears from prominence in American politics. Presidents who have lost bids for reelection (Jimmy Carter in 1980; George Bush in 1992) do not play the role of leader of the opposition. They are occasionally consulted because of their experience and expertise, but mostly, they are retired and replaced by a new generation of leaders. Bob Dole, who had been a Republican leader in the Senate for three decades, left his seat in the Senate when he ran for president in 1996. No one clamored for him to return to the Senate to lead the Republican opposition. Nowadays, he is most prominently seen as a pitchman for Viagra on TV ads.

Again, if there is no glory for a second-place finisher, there is less for those who finished third, fourth, or fifth. In parliamentary systems, those who poll well, even if they lose, might well be rewarded with seats at the Cabinet table. Thus, the Free Democrats and the Greens have been rewarded with the foreign ministry after the recent German elections. If their votes are needed for the government to form a majority, they might well have a good deal of influence and be able to gain policy concessions. In Israel the ultrareligious parties have successfully used the influence accruing from their few seats in this manner. Such incentives can be more than enough for a party to continue, even with little hope of winning outright control. But in our system, losing candidates and their parties are not rewarded, and thus electoral frustration is total.

If one looks at gubernatorial elections, at elections to either house of Congress, or at elections to state legislatures, a similar pattern appears. As mentioned earlier, almost all of these elections are run under plurality-winner, first-past-the-post rules. One candidate is the winner; no prize goes to the "place" or "show" finisher. Third-party candidates might play the role of spoiler, but they rarely win.

After the 2000 elections, Bernie Sanders from Vermont and Virgil Goode from Virginia are the only non-major party members of Congress; they caucus with the major parties in the House (Sanders with the Democrats; Goode, who left the Democratic party, with the Republicans) and are dependent upon them for committee assignments. In Sanders's long career, he has not had a Democratic opponent in his biennial elections; Goode did not face a Republican opponent in his first run as an independent in 2000. All other third-party candidates have lost, and their parties have received no rewards for contesting the election, even if their participation affected the result. In the U.S. Senate, Jim Jeffords from Vermont is the only independent, but he left the Republican party after his last reelection; he was given his committee assignments by the Democrats.

Again, the American experience contrasts markedly with systems using proportional representation, as in Israel, in which each party is awarded seats in the legislature in proportion to the votes it receives in the election. And as already noted, if no party wins a majority in the legislature in systems like this, minor parties are invited into coalitions in order to form a majority, thereby significantly enhancing their influence and their incentive to persevere.

Although we believe that the structural and institutional arrangements in place for American elections make it difficult for third parties to arise, we are also mindful that "no electoral system can protect major political parties from the electorate" (Abramson et al., 1995:366–367). Even expressing the proposition in this way should alert readers that the dilemma is highly nuanced. We are talking about the preservation of two-party politics in which the Democrats and the Republicans remain the two dominant parties, as they have for nearly 150 years. We believe that this system is likely to remain in place. But if it were to be altered, it could be altered in one of two very different directions.

One type of alteration would be for a new party to emerge to replace one of the existing parties—and for a new two-party system to become established that way. That is essentially what happened in the period between 1856 and 1860 when the Republicans replaced the Whigs in American politics. For a brief period of time, more than two parties vied for power, but when the dust settled, two-party democracy remained (Sundquist, 1983).

We do not see that scenario arising. The Republican and Democratic parties have shown a remarkable ability to adapt to changing political dialogue in the years since they began competing with each other. As new issues have arisen, new parties have come along to voice concerns. But when those voices have reached a crescendo, the Republicans and Democrats have altered their own policy views to take into account the opinions of those who would support alternative parties (recall Chapter 2). These adaptations can be observed most noticeably in politics at the time of the so-called critical elections of 1896 and 1932, but they were also in evidence during the Progressive Era and at other times. As organizations, the two major parties have a stake in self-preservation and have wisely adapted in order to continue to exist. The budget and tax-cut negotiations between President Clinton and the Democrats on one side and the Republicans controlling the Congress on the other provide a good example. During summer 1997, both parties compromised significantly in order to avoid the gridlock and government shutdown of the first Clinton term, an effort that provides evidence that the parties are again adapting to the concerns expressed by prominent third-party candidates (in this case Ross Perot and the Reform party).

The other type of alteration would be moving from a two-party system to a multiparty system. Those who favor a three-party or a multiparty system argue that two parties cannot possibly reflect the breadth of opinion in a country as diverse as the United States. Thus, they conclude that citizens are bound to be frustrated with the results of two-party politics. They also argue that the two parties are so intent on not alienating any bloc of citizens that they do not have the ability to address the nation's most pressing problems. In our view, these critics of two-party politics, including those who predict its demise, are in error. *We believe that the history of two-party politics in this nation, a history that emerged as it did for reasons spelled out here earlier, provides ample evidence that such a system is compatible with this nation's society, culture, and governmental structure. We see no evidence that it is about to change. Moreover, we do not believe that it should.*

A Defense of Two-Party Politics in America

Undesirable Institutional Consequences of Multipartyism

We begin our normative defense of the two-party system by noting those political institutions that support such a system. If one concedes that these institutions make it difficult for third parties to continue to exist, as we argued in Chapter 3, then one must argue that they should be eliminated in order to make multiparty democracy possible. Do we really want to follow that course?

Let us begin with the *separation of powers*. No aspect of American democracy is more fundamental than the separation of the executive power from the legislative power (and from the judicial power, though that is less relevant for our purposes). Separation of powers and the checks and balances that follow from this separation were thought by the founders to be a sine qua non for limited government. Nothing in the more than two hundred years of the American experiment in democracy has shaken that faith. We remain convinced that all power concentrated in the hands of those controlling the government would violate our most basic tenets of democracy.

But separate election of the chief executive from that of the national legislature, with overlapping terms, as exists in our system, creates an obvious incentive to form broad-based parties capable of winning the most important prize in the electoral system, the presidency. Multiparty systems are more compatible with parliamentary forms of government that permit the possibility of cross-party coalitions forming to select the chief executive. We do not believe that Americans would sacrifice the constitutional safety implied in separation of powers for whatever promises a multiparty system might hold.

We believe that much the same argument can be made for other aspects of the current system that would require drastic revision for a three- or multiparty system to replace the current two-party domination. Multiparty systems thrive in electoral environments defined by proportional representation and the concept of more than one representative elected from each constituency for the same office. Geographic representation is thus diluted.

The American system of *single-member districts with plurality winners*, used for electing U.S. representatives and senators and for most governors and state legislators, works to the disadvantage of minor parties that have little chance of winning any of these offices, much less of gaining influence in the national or state legislatures. Without the incentive of gaining influence, third parties are less likely to contest offices in a serious manner up and down the ballot over a period of years.

We must remember that one of the principles on which our system rests is geographic representation. We as a nation believe that we should be represented by those who live among us. At the time of the founding, congressional districts contained relatively small populations. Although district populations routinely exceed half a million today, we hold to the myth that our representatives are looking out for our local interests as if all districts were still homogeneous. In many states, legislative districts remain small. A move to a system of proportional representation, which would provide the context for a multiparty system, would necessitate giving up local representation.

Imagine the political dialogue over a constitutional amendment saying that we would no longer have local representation in Congress and in our state legislatures but rather would have the entire legislature elected in larger geographic regions so that minor parties could get representation. Who wins in your state? Which regions would lose their representation because of smaller populations? How would this kind of change affect rural areas, minority groups, and areas that are distinct and isolated from their state's population centers, such as upstate New York, downstate Illinois, or the Upper Peninsula of Michigan? The concept of calling on "our own" representative to argue for the interests of our own area is deeply embedded in the American political psyche. Again, we do not see any likelihood that citizens would jump to change this institutional aspect of the system in order to set the stage for multiparty electoral contests.

Direct primary elections and the complex *presidential primary system* that has evolved in the last two decades also work to reinforce two-party electoral competition. Although public commitment to these aspects of our electoral process is not as strong as it is to separation of powers or single-member geographic representation, no realistic reformer is suggesting that we go back to a system in which party bosses dominate the nominating process. Yet that is precisely what happens in multiparty systems. Party leaders create slates of candidates from whom the electorate chooses; the candidates are ranked so that those higher on the list have a better chance of election (depending on the proportion of the vote the party receives and therefore the number of candidates who are elected).

The direct primary system was an innovation of the Progressive Era, a way reformers found for taking power from the party bosses and giving it back to the people. But the primary system has had the unintended consequence of allowing those who are at the fringes of American public opinion to work within the two-party framework to gain influence. It is much easier for someone to capture a primary election than it is to form a separate political party or run as an independent.

The direct primary system and the presidential nominating process make American parties open and susceptible to domination (or even capture) by those out of the ideological mainstream. Primary electorates are small and unique in each state; because primaries are spread throughout a number of months and held at different times in different states, they do not receive concentrated media attention. Thus, a fringe group, composed of the supporters of Lyndon LaRouche, was able to capture statewide nominations for lieutenant governor and secretary of state in Illinois in 1982. Antiabortion forces gained ground in many states by defeating prochoice candidates in primaries. The same can be said of environmentalists, antitax groups, and others with particular agenda items. Passionate interests can dominate in elections, such as primaries, that are marked with low voter turnout. The openness of the primary system encourages candidates who might form minor parties in other political systems to work to capture one of the two major parties—and thus have the opportunity to win election—in ours; it thus reduces the incentives for minor parties to form and contest for office (Epstein, 1986:244–245).

Similarly, the presidential primary system allowed a Barry Goldwater to capture the Republican nomination in 1964, when his conservative views were considered far out of the mainstream, and it allowed a George McGovern to be nominated by the Democrats in 1972, this time representing anti–Vietnam War policies and social views far more liberal than those of most Democrats. In recent years, the Reverend Jesse Jackson has chosen to compete within the framework of the Democratic party rather than convert the Rainbow Coalition into a minor political party. In like manner, Gary Bauer, whose conservative social views are more doctrinaire than those of most Republicans, felt that he could have more influence by competing in Republican primaries and seeking his party's nomination than by forming a third party for the general election. It is ironic that the very openness of the primary system—at the national and local level—that makes it difficult for party leaders to control the direction of their own organizations also discourages the formation of additional parties to challenge Republican and Democratic party domination. Again, we see little evidence that Americans want to give up the open and participatory nominating systems currently in place in order to encourage the formation of additional political parties.

We should add that other aspects of the current electoral system that are less popular than those just mentioned would also require significant modification were a multiparty system to replace the current two-party competition. Specifically, the Electoral College, which many believe to be outmoded, is not compatible with a multiparty system in its current format; the Federal Election Campaign Act clearly favors major parties by allocating more funds to them than to minor parties; and ballot access laws, including the so-called sore loser laws, in most states would require significant amendment. Although the public would not rush to the defense of any of these aspects of the current system, one should not underestimate the difficulty reformers would face in finding acceptable alternatives. It is far easier to foster public opinion against an aspect of the current system than it is to form a coalition in favor of a specific way of amending it.

Accountability Under Two-Party Competition

If a democracy is to function acceptably, citizens must have a mechanism for rewarding those elected officials whose work they approve of and replacing those whose performance is found lacking. Elected officials, who generally seek to remain in office, understand this basic tenet of democracy and thus work hard to satisfy the demands of their constituents.

Some aspects of American democracy work against the principle of accountability. Most notably, the separation of powers, especially in cases where one party controls the executive and the other the legislature, and the federal system, in which one party might well be in control of a citizen's state government and the other party of the national government, obscure responsibility and thus make accountability difficult to achieve. In addition, it is difficult to hold individuals accountable because of the lack of internal unity within our political parties; public officials elected under the same party's banner often have diverse and even conflicting views on important policy areas. Nonetheless, because of the two-party system, accountability in our system is made easier than it would be if many parties were in competition for control of the government.

In this case the question involves how much information one believes citizens need in order to hold public officials accountable. If one thinks that an informed citizenry must have detailed information on all aspects of the functioning of its government and on policy alternatives proposed by those seeking office in order to hold elected officials accountable for their actions, our democracy fails. However, if one accepts a different test—that citizens must simply be able to assess whether they are satisfied with the general direction of government policy in the areas that are of concern to them—then our two-party system serves the accountability criterion of democracy quite well.

In every election, candidates and parties express their views on an impressive variety of issues. Voters find themselves in agreement with some candidates on some issues and with others on other issues, but each citizen has only one vote for president, one vote for each office on the ballot. Elections thus do not allow voters to render judgments on specific issues, but they can express their views of performance in office. In 1980, the voters said clearly to President Jimmy Carter that they did not like the direction he and the Democrats were leading the nation. In 1992, the voters sent a similar message to the Republicans and to George Bush. And in 1994, they sent a clarion call to the Democrats, who had controlled the Congress for forty years, that their performance in office was no longer acceptable. A two-party system permits this kind of retrospective performance analysis in a way that would be impossible with many parties competing for control. In so doing, it serves the purposes of our representative democracy.

Policy Implementation Under Two-Party Politics

Those seeking alternatives to the two-party system say that it is flawed because of an inability to govern effectively. Some, such as Theodore Lowi (1996:47), say that because the parties must make such broad appeals, they promise too many things to too many people and are thus immobilized. Others claim that intense partisanship leads to policy gridlock, at least under circumstances of divided government. We disagree on all counts. In our view, a two-party system enhances the opportunity for effective government in a constitutional system marked by separation of powers and federalism.

First, we must concede that policymaking is difficult under our system of government. We should also remember that that difficulty was an intentional consequence of the system established by the founders. They did not want a government that ran roughshod over the citizenry. Policymaking within a framework such as that established by our Constitution requires extensive negotiation, bargaining, compromise, and cross-party coalition building (Brady and Buckley, 1994, 1998, 2002). Government can be deadlocked by institutional or partisan bickering, as was demonstrated at the national level in 1995 when the government was forced to shut down because of the failure to pass a budget reconciliation bill on which the Democratic president and the Republican Congress could agree.

It is difficult for us to imagine how introducing a substantial number of third- or fourth-party representatives into the Congress would alleviate this kind of situation. Deadlock in parliaments with multiparty systems has led to the collapse of government after government, with no resolution of the pending issues. But in our system, marked by elections at regular intervals and no votes of confidence that can lead to calls for new elections, the protracted negotiations that would be necessary to form even transitory coalitions would make the pace of government policymaking unbearably slow. Extremist elements in our society could well gain enhanced influence on a range of issues if their parties' support were necessary to organize a legislative chamber (e.g., if no one party had a majority) or merely to pass critical legislation.

A system with more parties in the legislature implies that those parties would be smaller and that their appeal would be narrower. One logical consequence would be the formation of parties around polarized views on highly salient issues, for example, abortion or affirmative action. The legislative representatives of these parties would be far less likely than those of broad-based parties to compromise and to cross party lines in order to push forward the national agenda. Cohesive, polarized legislative parties could only contribute to intensified conflict, greater divisiveness, extended delay, and gridlock.

What if the representative of one of these parties achieved the ultimate prize in our system, the presidency? And what if that president had to deal with a Congress dominated by Democrats and Republicans? This scenario is a more likely one under a transition to the multiparty system that some see emerging in the United States today. We see it as a recipe for disaster. Imagine a Ross Perot negotiating with the Republicans and Democrats, whom he so enjoyed denouncing during his two campaigns for the presidency. But one does not have to imagine. Go to Connecticut or Alaska and ask citizens there about the effectiveness of Governor Weicker or Governor Hickel in dealing with their legislatures. Gridlock and acrimony dominate legislative sessions in both states.

To be fair, one would get very different answers if one were to go to Maine and discuss the effectiveness of Governor King with his legislature. But in a very real sense, the exception proves our point. King argued from the start that he was not opposed to the two parties but instead looked forward to working with them. He did not form his own party, nor did others run for the legislature in the election halfway through his term as representatives of his organization. He presented himself as an independent, not a third-party candidate; his appeal was to bridge the gap between the two major parties and end the bickering, not to replace them.

We do not grant the premise of critics that under two-party politics, effective government is not possible. To the contrary, our view is that elections under this system matter—and they matter a great deal when the public has reached a consensus on the direction policy should take. Thus, the Great Society social programs followed Lyndon Johnson's landslide election in 1964. But when Johnson seemed to be pushing the government too fast, the public reacted and elected a large number of Republicans to Congress in 1966. Government retrenchment and the beginning of devolution of responsibilities to the states resulted from Ronald Reagan's victory in 1980; but again the Republican revolution was slowed before it gained too much momentum by Democratic congressional victories in 1982. Charles O. Jones, a former president of the American Political Science Association and a longtime student of parties, the presidency, and the Congress, has commented that ours is the "greatest self-adjusting" political system in existence.

Look at the impact of recent elections. The Democrats returned to unified control of the national government in 1992, but the public felt that President Clinton tried to go too far, too fast, particularly on health care. The Republicans swept to overwhelming victories in the 1994 congressional elections, regaining control of the House for the first time in forty years and of the Senate for the first time in eight. They attempted to implement the Contract with America, a Republican policy revolution, but they, too, seemed to go too far, too fast.

Perhaps the most significant aspect of the Democratic victory in 1992 and the Republican victory in the congressional elections of 1994—and the Republicans' retaining control of both houses of Congress in the 1996 election, despite President Clinton's overwhelming reelection victory—was that these mixed results led directly to bargaining and compromise between leaders of the two parties as they faced budget negotiations in the 105th Congress in 1997. The elections led to policy changes, but not radical changes, as the next election presaged self-adjustment.

When George W. Bush won the 2000 election, and the Republicans controlled both houses of Congress, some felt that unified party control of the two branches would lead to partisan policymaking. But the narrowness of Bush's win and of the Republican margins in the Congress—a margin that disappeared when Senator Jeffords left the GOP and became an independent during the first session of the 107th Congress—meant that Republican policy initiatives faced tough sledding in the legislature. The events of September 11, 2001, led to a period of bipartisan rhetoric and unity behind the president's efforts to respond to the attacks and to protect the nation, but the fight in Congress over whether airport security personnel should be federal employees demonstrated for everyone that compromise would still be necessary.

We see these examples of compromise as positive examples of effective government under two-party politics that would certainly have been more difficult, if not impossible, had a significant number of third- or fourth-party legislators or a president representing neither of the two major parties been introduced into the mix.

Legitimacy and Policy Moderation Under Two-Party Politics

In their most recent quadrennial assessment of presidential elections, political scientists Nelson W. Polsby and the late Aaron Wildavsky noted that the Electoral College has the hidden impact of restricting the number of effective political parties to two. Like us, they assess this restriction positively: "This helps focus the electorate on a limited menu of choices. In turn, this increases the chance that winners will have the backing of a sizable number of voters and the legitimacy to lead Congress and the nation" (2000:248–9).

Similarly, the first-past-the-post winner provision of most other elections for national or state legislators and for state executives, principally contested by the Republicans and the Democrats, also guarantees that the winner will have won the support of either a majority or a sizable plurality of the voters. Vote totals of significant magnitude add an aura of legitimacy to election-day winners, even in relatively close elections.

Consider the following comparison. In Case A, the winner polls 49 percent of the vote; the runner-up, 46 percent of the vote; and minor party candidates 2 percent, 2 percent, and 1 percent respectively. In Case B, the winner polls 26 percent of the vote; the runner-up, 23 percent; and additional party candidates 20 percent, 20 percent, and 5 percent respectively. The margin between the top two candidates is 3 percent in each case. But in Case A, the winner would have polled nearly a majority and would have received nearly twenty-five times as many votes as the nearest minor party candidate, whereas in Case B, the top two minor party candidates together would have polled nearly one and one-half times as many votes as the winner. We think it obvious that the winner in Case A would be able to speak for his or her constituents with a much more legitimate mandate than would the winner in Case B. Furthermore, of course, if our system resembled Case B, the alternative party candidates would be encouraged to run more and more serious campaigns, with the result that election outcomes would always show fragmentation. The mechanism through which the two-party system instills the winner with a mantle of legitimacy is by encouraging various groups that could serve to fragment the polity to compromise and come together with others with whom they share some points of view under the umbrella of one or the other of the major parties.

In so doing, the two-party system all but necessitates that the major parties be centrist and moderate; they can only succeed if they can appeal to a wide variety of people. Critics complain that the parties are like Mungojerrie and Rumplteazer, the indistinguishable felines who cause all sorts of mischief in the Broadway musical *Cats*. We believe these critics mistake a strength of the two-party system for a weakness. In today's highly charged political atmosphere—characterized by attack ads during campaigns, volatile criticism of all incumbents by talk radio hosts, ideological standards for morality, and emphasis on salient, emotional single issue politics—it is the political parties that seek to build consensus, that seek to minimize the potential for our society to split itself asunder. It is also the political parties that give representation to sometimes unpopular minority groups that otherwise would be further disenfranchised and marginalized. And it is the moderate, centrist, nonideological two-party system that has done so successfully on all but one occasion, the Civil War, throughout this nation's entire history.

For generations, political scientists have noted this feature of American political parties. In the 1940s, John Fischer distinguished American parties, whose purpose is "not to divide but unite," from European parties, whose purpose is "to divide men of different ideologies into coherent and disciplined organizations" (Fischer, 1948:32). In the 1950s, Willmore Kendall and Austin Ranney, authors of the leading textbook of their day, noted that "the party system, more than any other American institution . . . consciously, actively, and directly nurtures consensus" (Kendall and Ranney, 1956:509). In the 1960s, V. O. Key Jr., the leading scholar of American political parties in the post–World War II era, noted that "given . . . [the] tendency for most people to cluster fairly closely together in their attitudes, a dual division becomes possible. . . . Extremists exist . . . but they never seem to be numerous enough or intransigent enough to form the bases for durable minor parties" (Key, 1964:210).

Critics of the two-party system stress the necessity for all segments of our society to be able to vote for someone who reflects their particular nuanced point of view. In a multiparty system, those views could be represented on election day, but they would not be more accurately reflected in policies adopted. Rather than attempts at national unity, reconciliation, and policy moderation, we would have a polity noted for divisiveness, acrimony, and extremism. Multiparty systems are often marked by instability and frequent, radical changes in policy directions. We prefer the former to the latter. When a moderate party system proved incapable of handling a divisive schism that split this nation, "to the astonishment of each side, the North and South found themselves at war" (Brogan, 1954:513).

Although the issues of today may not seem as volatile, we should not lose sight of the role the two-party system plays in calming emotions. The major parties each desire to win. To win in the American context, each must have widespread support and appeal to the wide variety of interests that constitute this nation. In searching for support from that median voter whose allegiance is necessary to secure victory, the Democrats and the Republicans may not quite please anyone, but neither do they create situations so intolerable for the losing side that continuing to seek proximate solutions to pressing social problems through political means seems unreasonable. Critics complain that the Democrats and the Republicans are so concerned with winning that the battles of American politics are fought "within the forty-yard lines" of the ideological football field. We agree with their assessment and are thankful that winners are not so far removed from losers that those who fail in one political battle feel they must fight the next round through other means.

Summary

Our conclusions on the first two questions with which we began this chapter are clear. *We believe that the American two-party system is likely to continue into the next century. And we believe that that is a good thing.* A system that has persisted for more than two centuries, for nearly a century and a half with little transformation, that is sustained by fundamental institutions basic to our form of government, that serves the needs of a democracy to hold public officials accountable to the electorate, and that gives legitimacy to the efforts of those public officials as they seek reconciliation and unity on the issues that divide a vast and diverse nation should not be discarded lightly. The onus is still on the critics to demonstrate that the polity would function as effectively under a system in which three or more parties contest competitively for national office. We do not believe that they have met that test to this point.

Reforming the Two-Party System

Recall the dilemma that structures this book. Americans have a certain ambivalence about the two-party system, yet it has persisted throughout the nation's history. We have argued that the persistence of two-party competition is understandable and that it is desirable for a variety of reasons. Thus, we could claim to have resolved the dilemma. But surely something is lacking. It cannot be healthy in a democracy for the citizenry to feel negatively about one of the primary institutional functions of that system. Thus, to conclude this book, we intend to discuss some steps that might be taken to improve the way we as citizens view the two-party system that structures our politics.

It is our belief that citizens become dissatisfied with the two-party system when it stops doing that which it does best—reconciling differences, taking steps toward national unity, seeking and finding consensus. We also believe that citizens become dissatisfied when those in government fail to confront the pressing issues of the day. And there is ample evidence that citizens are concerned about the means of politics—particularly about the ways in which political parties finance their campaigns. In recent years, each of these causes has contributed to the ways in which Americans view their parties and to the rise of third-party and independent candidacies.

In the mid-1950s, one could argue that dissatisfaction with the functioning of our two-party system arose because the parties, and thus the government, failed to deal with the pressing issue of the day, civil rights. In the late 1960s and early 1970s, the parties, and thus the government, failed to deal with the unpopularity of the war in Vietnam. Each of these was a period when dissidents sought means outside the two-party system to achieve political ends. But in each case the parties eventually responded, albeit not to the complete satisfaction of anyone but in a way in which everyone felt progress was made.

Those eras seem far removed from the current one. The common thread is that once again the government for some time has not responded to the issue of the day. Right or wrong, citizens have become concerned about increasing government indebtedness, about the stability of the Social Security system, about the solvency of Medicare and Medicaid. At a basic level, the public does not feel that elected representatives are living in the "real" world. The House bank scandal of 1992 symbolized this dissatisfaction. No public money was lost in that scandal, but the reputation of those in Congress suffered appreciably. Why? People felt that because we all have to balance our checkbooks, members of Congress should also have to. And the same argument has been held up for the federal government. We have to live within our individual means. And the government should, too.

Cynicism has built from there. Not only is the government not living within its means, but also it is taxing us at levels that are too high, and we no longer believe that it is capable of delivering the services on which we once counted –particularly health and financial security in our old age—and we sense that we cannot maintain the quality of life we have today. That cynicism has been directed at politicians who seem out to feather their own nests, who have been involved in various examples of petty corruption, who demonstrate more concern with their own reelection than with solving the nation's problems, and who spend more time fighting with each other than dealing with the nation's business.

The controversy over campaign financing in the 1996 and 2000 elections illustrates that point. The public sees clearly that the Federal Election Campaign Act is riddled with so many loopholes that no one is satisfied with how money is raised for politics. But the political parties each claim that they want reform more than the other—and little progress is made. Campaign finance reform is a difficult area in which to pass effective public policy. What is necessary is to pass a bill that allows for adequate communication between candidates and voters and does not violate the free speech provisions of the First Amendment but at the same time restricts some of the behavior that citizens reject as outlandish. Bipartisan cooperation would be needed to rid the system of some of its worst flaws, but those involved in this debate—party officials and those in the Congress—seem more intent on casting blame than on finding even partial solutions, such as tightening Federal Election Commission definitions of which advertisements are exempt from regulation, providing free television time for candidates, requiring more prompt reporting of receipts and expenditures, and restricting the amount of soft money that parties can expend. Not responding to an obvious need for reform detracts from the credibility of those who cannot address pressing problems in which they have a direct interest (Mann and Ornstein, 1994).[4]

Ross Perot drew on similar kinds of dissatisfaction in the rhetoric of his two campaigns. So did Lowell Weicker in Connecticut, Walter Hickel in Alaska, Angus King in Maine, and Jesse Ventura in Minnesota. But the dissatisfaction has another cause that relates more to how the parties are acting internally than to the functioning of the government.

To be successful, the major parties in a two-party system must appeal to the center of the political spectrum. We have argued that the necessity for moderation is one of the strengths of our system. But in recent years, the Democrats and the Republicans have allowed fringe elements within their coalitions to gain prominence. As a result, the acrimony in political rhetoric has risen. Not only are the parties not solving the nation's problems, but they are also failing to do so while engaging in behavior that most citizens reject.

In earlier eras, even as political leaders struggled with pressing issues of the day, periods when comity broke down within the halls of government were rare. Democrats and Republicans might have disagreed, but they were rarely disagreeable. Even as late as the 1980s, Republican president Ronald Reagan and Democratic Speaker of the House Thomas P. "Tip" O'Neill—partisans who disagreed on virtually every philosophical issue before the government—sat down and discussed their disagreements calmly and with respect for each other.

Today, the opposite seems to be true. The 1990s were marked by moderate leaders' leaving the Senate—like Democratic senators Bill Bradley (NJ), Tim Wirth (CO), and Sam Nunn (GA) and Republican senators Warren Rudman (NH), Nancy Kassebaum (KS), and William Cohen (ME)—in part because it is no longer a place in which they like to work. When they were in the minority, the Republicans, led by Newt Gingrich of Georgia before he became a party leader, used the one-minute speeches on the House floor at the end of the day as a medium for attacking Democrats. The Democrats responded in kind. Even in the post-Gingrich House of Representatives, the Republican Speaker and the Democratic leader rarely consult each other and have a relationship characterized by

hostility and mistrust. Each side has claimed the moral high ground and has attacked the other, not as political opposition but as an enemy to be vanquished.
Observers of the news on television have come to expect negative responses to
every proposal—from both the Republican administration and the Democrats in
Congress—before time for any thoughtful analysis has been possible. And the
public response to this has been overwhelmingly negative.

A second factor should be added to this partisan acrimony. Although the two
parties have traditionally understood the need to be moderate in order to attract a
majority share of the electorate, in recent years each has come to rely heavily on its
extreme wing to stimulate voter turnout. The impact of these appeals has been to
exacerbate partisan differences rather than to seek reconciliation. Thus, the Democrats have relied on African-American leaders, led by Jesse Jackson, to build up
their popular vote totals. Similarly, the Republicans have opened their appeals to
the religious right—and built majorities in areas in which those groups dominate.
These internal party strains have had an effect on how each party expresses its
message and deals with its own constituents. Democratic liberals decried compromises proposed by President Clinton; doctrinaire conservatives in the House attempted a coup against Speaker Gingrich because they felt he had lost the message.

To the extent that the parties are dominated by their own extreme wings, they
divide rather than unify the nation. To the extent that political discourse is acri-
monious and not accommodating, the public becomes increasingly put off by the
process. Each of these gives rise to the dissatisfaction with politics as usual—with
the two-party politics we have been observing.

We believe that solutions are possible and that positive signs can be seen. In
summer 1997, President Clinton and the Republican leaders of the Congress negotiated a deal on balancing the budget and giving tax relief to many American
citizens. In negotiating that deal, partisans on both sides of the political aisle
praised the work of the opposition. Compromise was the watchword of the day.
"We gave ground, and the Administration gave ground, and we found common
ground," commented Republican Senate leader Trent Lott (MS) (*Congressional
Quarterly*, 1997:1832). President Clinton, who started his day at a White House
breakfast with Speaker Gingrich, added, "Final Congressional passage of the balanced budget bill is the achievement of a generation and a triumph for every
American" (*New York Times*, August 1, 1997).

In the midst of the negotiations that led to the agreement, doctrinaire conservatives within the House Republican party attempted a coup against Speaker Gingrich. The Speaker survived, with the assistance of moderate Republicans. The
Speaker's problems within the Republican Conference went deeper than ideological purity, but the fact that the moderates in the House asserted their power is
most significant. Similarly, a vast majority of the Democrats voted for the budget

plan, despite the fact that many of the party's leading liberals, including Minority Leader Richard Gephardt (MO) and David Obey (WI), the ranking Democrat on the Appropriations Committee, felt that President Clinton compromised excessively on a wide array of issues. For the Democrats supporting the compromise, moderation was the order of the day.

We see this kind of negotiation and agreement—and the effort to reassert power by moderates on both sides—as a positive step toward reestablishing faith in the two-party system. But it is clearly only one step. The level of political rhetoric must be reined in. Morality plays in politics divide a nation, because the stakes of the game become so much more fundamental, and the context then becomes different: When you lose, the government deems you to be morally flawed. That is unacceptable to most of us—and it is not the role we believe the government should be playing.

Political parties are successful when they define the issues that the public thinks the government should be dealing with and when they seek solutions to those problems. This country has been built on the principle that the government should not dominate our lives. Rather, the government should seek a better life for all citizens. The parties' role is to seek a consensus on what that means for today. When they are doing that—and when government policies reflect that consensus—then politicians are viewed more positively and politics are within acceptable bounds. That is the direction leaders should seek as our two-party system enters the twenty-first century.

Discussion Questions

Chapter 1

1. What are the most important roles that political parties play in a democracy?
2. How did Ross Perot's organization in the 1992 presidential election differ from his party in the 1996 election?
3. What do you think Americans are looking for in third-party or independent candidates?
4. Why do you think third parties and independent candidates seem to have more success in state elections than in national elections?

Chapter 2

1. What common traits do you find among the third parties that emerged in this country's first century of existence?
2. Why do you think the Republican party succeeded in achieving major party status while so many other third parties fell by the wayside?
3. What is meant by an electoral realignment? How do realignments relate to the role that parties play in a democratic system?
4. What has been the importance of third parties in American political history? How have they effected change in this nation's politics?
5. How has divided government impacted on the public's desire for more choice at the polls?
6. Discuss how the experiences of third parties in the various states differ from those of national third parties.

Chapter 3

1. What historical conditions in the United States encouraged the development of a two-party system?
2. Discuss the ways in which various institutional aspects of the American system of government impede the development of a multiparty system.
3. How persuasive is the evidence that the American public really wants a third major party to appear?
4. What aspects of the American political system do you see as most hostile to the development of a third major political party? Why?

5. Is the benefit of the Electoral College helping to promote two-party politics sufficient to compensate for the possibility that a president can be elected without winning a plurality of the popular vote?
6. Would democracy and representative government in the United States be better served if we abandoned single-member congressional and legislative districts in favor of a system of proportional representation?
7. Under what conditions might a new party arise to challenge the duopoly of the Republicans and the Democrats? Are those conditions likely to be present in the foreseeable future?

Chapter 4

1. What do you think is the best evidence indicating that Americans were expressing discontent at the ballot box in the elections in the early 1990s? Was there also substantial voter discontent in the 2000 elections?
2. How would you characterize the response of politicians to the public's expressions of discontent with the political system and with the alternatives they have been offered?
3. What are the main causes of public discontent? How do third parties address or fail to address these causes?
4. How would you evaluate the experiences with alternatives to two-party dominance that have occurred in Alaska, Connecticut, Maine, and Minnesota?

Chapter 5

1. Do you believe that the United States will continue to have a two-party system or that a third party will become a permanent feature of our politics?
2. What is the best argument you can make for a two-party system? What is the best argument for a three- or multiparty system? Which is more persuasive to you?
3. If you were asked to advise the chairs of the Democratic and Republican National Committees on how best to reform the existing system in order to meet public expectations, what advice would you give?

Glossary

Australian Ballot: This was a reform of the ballot instituted by the states in the 1890s under which the government printed and distributed ballots at the polling place. It replaced the system of each party printing its own ballots and distributing them to the voters. It was designed to reduce election-day fraud, but it also worked to the disadvantage of new parties seeking ballot access.

Ballot Access: The rules specified in each state by which candidates' names appear on the election ballot. Typically, the candidates of the major political parties are automatically given access to the ballot, whereas other parties' candidates or independent candidates must have achieved a prescribed threshold in a previous election or collect a specified number of signatures on a petition in order to appear.

Cross-filing: The practice of allowing one candidate's name to appear on more than one party's line on election-day ballots. Rules that permit cross-filing enhance the influence of minor parties.

Democratic and Republican "Leaners": Voters who respond to survey questions by saying that they do not feel committed to one party or the other but rather that they most frequently lean in that party's direction when casting their ballots.

Direct Primary: An election through which those who are affiliated with a particular party vote on whom that party should nominate for a particular office. Direct primaries vary according to how the eligible electorate is defined, with closed primaries restricting voting to those who declare party membership in one way or another and open primaries allowing all citizens to vote in whichever party's primary they choose. A few states (Alaska, California, and Washington) have had an even more open system, known as a blanket primary, in which all candidates for nomination appear on one ballot and citizens can vote for a Democrat for some offices and a Republican for others, and perhaps for a minor party candidate for still others. The U.S. Supreme Court declared California's blanket primary unconstitutional in 2000.

Divided Government: The situation in which the president of the United States is from one major political party and the majority of one or both houses of the Congress is from the other major political party.

Doctrinaire Parties: Minor parties noted for their strict adherence to certain philosophical or policy positions on which they will not compromise regardless of electoral consequences, e.g., the Socialist Workers party.

Electoral College: The system through which the president and vice president of the United States are elected. Each state is awarded a number of electoral votes equal to the number of representatives and senators representing that state in the U.S. Congress.

On election day, citizens actually vote for electors pledged to support the candidate of their choice. In all states except Maine and Nebraska, all of the electoral votes go to whichever candidate's electors win a plurality of the votes cast. (How electoral votes are to be allocated is provided for by state law. In Maine and Nebraska, plurality winners in each congressional district are awarded one electoral vote and the statewide winner is awarded two.) The winner of the presidency is the candidate who receives a majority of the electoral votes cast throughout the nation. If no candidate wins such a majority, the House of Representatives decides the winner from among the top three finishers.

Federal Election Campaign Act (FECA): The law, first passed in 1971 and significantly amended in 1974 and in less important ways on a number of occasions since then, that specifies how federal elections are to be financed. Among the important provisions of the FECA are those that call for federal funding of presidential primaries on a matching funds basis, full federal funding of presidential general elections, and restrictions on the amounts of money individuals and groups can give to campaigns for federal offices.

First-Past-the-Post: The slang reference to an electoral system in which there is one winner in a particular district and that winner is the candidate who receives more votes than any other candidate, regardless of whether that vote total constitutes a majority.

Fusion: The combining of two or more party coalitions behind one candidate or group of candidates.

Independent: Not affiliated with any political party. Minor-party candidates, inaccurately, are often referred to as independent candidates. True independent candidates or voters eschew affiliation or allegiance with any political party.

Multiparty System: An electoral system in which more than two parties must take each other into account as they determine strategies, appeal to the electorate, and attempt to form governments.

National Conventions: The forums at which presidential and vice presidential candidates are nominated in the United States. Nominations are made by delegates to these conventions. Most delegates are elected in primary elections in the various states and territories, though some individuals are accorded delegate status by virtue of the positions they hold, e.g., members of the national committees, state party officers, or members of Congress.

New Deal Democratic Coalition: The groups that came together to support Franklin D. Roosevelt and the Democratic party after the 1932 election. The coalition, whose composition included groups such as Catholics and Jews, union members, blacks, liberal intellectuals, and Southerners, generally held together and supported Democratic candidates into the 1960s.

"New" Parties: Minor political parties that have drawn support from those concerned with political issues other than the traditional economic issues that have dominated politics, e.g., the Green party, which is concerned with environmental issues.

Nonpartisan Elections: Elections in which candidates do not contest for office under a party label. Many localities hold nonpartisan elections for offices from school board to mayor. Nebraska is the only state in which elections to the state legislature are held without candidates specifying party affiliation.

Party Identifiers: Those who respond to survey questions by saying that they generally consider themselves to be identified with or closer to one major political party or the other. This type of identification is a psychological affinity to a party, not a formal membership in that party. Most surveys ask respondents to specify whether they strongly identify with that political party or do so less strongly. Party identifiers are distinguished from those who lean toward one party or the other but do not feel that they really identify themselves as part of that party and from true independents, who do not lean in either direction, much less feel identification.

Party System: A pattern of interaction between or among political parties in which the parties must take each other into account as they choose their candidates, set their strategies, contest for office, and govern.

Presidential Debates: Well-publicized, nationally televised "debates" between or among the presidential candidates in the general election. These debates have been an important feature of recent presidential elections. One measure of a non-major party candidate's seriousness as a contender in the general election is whether or not that candidate is included in these debates.

Presidential Primary: The means used in most states to decide on delegations to national nominating conventions. Different states hold their primaries on different days, under different rules; and, in fact, the rules are often different between the Republicans and the Democrats, as each state and each party is permitted to set its own rules. Primaries are distinguished from systems in states that use a combination of caucuses (party meetings) and conventions (of delegates chosen at those caucuses) to select national convention delegates instead of holding statewide elections.

Proportional Representation: An electoral system in which candidates run under a party label and each party is allotted a number of seats in proportion to the number of votes it receives. In these elections, individual candidates are viewed as less important by the electorate than are parties. In the American system, proportional representation is used in some states for Republicans and in all states for Democrats in allocating delegates to the national nominating conventions for each of the contenders who contest presidential primaries.

Realignment: Fundamental change in voting coalitions and in the issues that divide the electorate.

Sectionalism: Voting based on region of the country rather than national concerns.

Single-member District System: An electoral system in which each defined constituency chooses only one representative. (See also First-Past-the-Post.)

Sore Loser Laws: Laws that prohibit those who lose the contest for a party's nomination from running in the general election as an independent candidate.

Splinter Candidacies: Candidates for office who break off from one of the major parties and take some of that party's natural constituency with them. A prime example was the States' Rights party candidacy of Strom Thurmond in 1948, when he broke from the Democratic party over the issue of civil rights and denied President Truman the electoral votes of southern states on which Democratic candidates had come to count.

Strategic Voting: Not voting for a candidate because one thinks that candidate's chances are doomed and that such a vote would dilute support from the real contender whose views are next closest to one's own.

Trial Balloon: Floating an idea in public, often through the media, before formally deciding to suggest it. Politicians use trial balloons to see if the public will react positively to an idea; they abandon those ideas that do not receive a warm reception without ever actually proposing them.

Two-Party System: An electoral system in which only two parties have real chances of success and thus must take only each other into account as they set strategies, choose candidates, contest for office, and govern.

Unicameral: One house or one body. Most legislatures in the United States have two houses, e.g., the U.S. Senate and the House of Representatives. The Nebraska state legislature and most city councils are unicameral, with only one body, not two.

United We Stand America: The group established by Ross Perot to support his candidacy in 1992. Major elements of United We Stand eventually merged into the Reform party.

Winner-Take-All: An electoral procedure under which the candidate who receives the most votes wins, as in the single-member district system for electing U.S. representatives and in allocating a state's electoral votes among presidential candidates.

Appendix: Significant Third Parties and Independent Candidates in American History

American Independent Party (George Wallace):   In 1968, the Democratic party was in the throes of internal controversy caused by the issues of civil rights, the Vietnam War, urban riots, and President Johnson's Great Society programs. George Wallace, the segregationist Democratic governor of Alabama, sought to take advantage of the tensions these issues had created, especially among white blue-collar voters, by running as splinter party candidate for president. Wallace carried five Deep South states and won 13.5 percent of the vote in 1968. Following the election, Wallace returned to the Democratic party, and the American Independent party collapsed after the 1976 election.

American (Know-Nothing) Party: The Know-Nothings were an anti-immigrant and anti-Catholic party that had considerable success in state elections in 1854 as the old Democratic-Whig party system was crumbling. The party acquired the name "Know-Nothing" because its members refused to reveal any information to outsiders about the party's secret rituals and greetings. As the divisions between the North and South intensified after the passage of the Kansas-Nebraska Act in 1854 and as the Republican party emerged, the nationalistic Know-Nothings faded out of existence.

Anderson, John B. (Independent Candidate, 1980):   After unsuccessfully seeking the Republican nomination for president, Anderson, a moderate GOP congressman from Illinois, ran for president as an independent. Although he had hoped to be a centrist choice between the conservative Republican nominee, Ronald Reagan, and President Jimmy Carter, a Democrat, his support and financial backing came primarily from liberals. Even though he lacked an emotional issue and was underfinanced and without a strong organization, Anderson was able to gain 6.6 percent of the vote. He retired from political life following the 1980 election.

Anti-Masonic Party: The Anti-Masons were an early-nineteenth-century manifestation of fundamentalist Christian distrust of the elite establishment and secularism. Emerging during the Jackson administration, the Anti-Masonic party was the first national third party and is best remembered for instituting the national convention in 1831 as the method for nominating presidential candidates. In 1833, it ceased to exist as a national entity and merged with the National Republicans to form the Whig party.

Bull Moose Progressive Party of 1912 (Theodore Roosevelt):   The Bull Moose party (officially, the National Progressive party) was Theodore Roosevelt's vehicle to reclaim the

White House after the Republican convention rejected him as its nominee in favor of President William Howard Taft in 1912. His candidacy also reflected a split between the conservative and progressive factions of the GOP. Roosevelt came in second in the popular vote. His candidacy split the Republican vote and enabled Democrat Woodrow Wilson to be elected with 42 percent of the vote. Following the election, Roosevelt returned to the Republican fold and endorsed its presidential nominee in 1916.

Conservative Party of New York State: This state-level minor party was formed in 1961 by dissident conservative Republicans who were dissatisfied with the moderate to liberal character of the Republican party that was dominated by Governor Nelson Rockefeller. The party's emergence and durability has been facilitated by New York's unique election law, which permits a candidate to appear on the ballot as the nominee of more than one party ("cross-filing"). The party had its greatest success in 1970, when its senatorial nominee, James Buckley, defeated the Republican and Democratic/Liberal party candidates. Normally, the Conservative party runs Republican nominees on its ballot line; cross-filing permits it to exert influence on the GOP by threatening to run its own candidate or to nominate the Democratic candidate.

Constitutional Union Party: In 1860, conservative Whigs, who opposed Abraham Lincoln's nomination by the Republicans, formed the Constitutional Union party. They believed that the Union could be preserved by taking no stand on the role of the national government in the expansion of slavery into the territories. The party's nominee, John Bell, carried only Virginia, Kentucky, and Tennessee. The party disappeared after the election of 1860, amid the secession of the southern states and the Civil War.

Farmer-Labor Party of Minnesota: The Farmer-Labor party began as a populist faction within the Minnesota Republican party. After failing to have a significant influence with the GOP, its reformist leaders in the 1920s formed a separate Farmer-Labor party. The party quickly became the principal electoral opposition to the dominant Republicans, and the Democratic party was reduced to third-party status in state politics. From 1930 through 1936, the Farmer-Labor candidates won the governorship. However, the pull of national political alignments overwhelmed the party during the 1940s, and in 1944, it merged into the Democratic party. Since then, the official name of the Minnesota Democrats has been the Democratic Farmer-Labor party (DFL).

Free Soil Party: Organized in 1848, the Free Soilers were the pragmatic successors to the antislavery Liberty party. They opposed extension of slavery in newly acquired territories and advocated a homestead act to provide land to settlers. By 1854, the party had been absorbed into the newly formed Republican party.

Green Party: The Greens are a minor party of the ideological left that gained considerable media attention in 1996 by nominating Ralph Nader, the longtime consumer and environmental activist, as its presidential candidate. Nader did not actively campaign but still received nearly 700,000 votes (.71 percent). The party again nominated Nader in 2000. This time with Nader campaigning aggressively on environmental, anticorporate, and anti–free trade themes, the party gained 2.7 percent of the vote. Most of the Nader votes came at the expense of the Democratic nominee, Vice President Al Gore. Most analysts believe that had Nader not been on the ballot, Gore would have carried some closely contested states such as Florida, New Hampshire, and Tennessee and thereby won an Electoral College majority. The Greens are illustrative of a "new" type of minor party composed of aggressive and dedicated activists that has emerged in recent years.

Greenback (National Independent) Party: The economic panic of 1873 was the driving force behind the emergence of this party of economic protest. It sought to unite hard-pressed farmers and urban workers through a platform that advocated issuance of paper currency to expand the money supply to provide needed capital for farmers, workers, and industries. In the midterm elections of 1878, it won over 1 million votes, but amid the return of economic prosperity and splits between its farm and labor factions after 1884, the party dissolved.

Liberal Party of New York State: This state-based party was formed in 1946 by garment industry union leaders who abandoned the American Labor party (ALP) after a long intraparty struggle for control with radical elements in that party. The Liberal party has relied primarily on support from garment workers, other unions, and Jewish voters in New York City. It has survived by taking advantage of New York's election laws that permit "cross-filing" and by endorsing major party candidates—usually Democrats—in return for concessions or, alternatively, by running its own candidate and therefore drawing votes away from the major parties. Since the 1970s, its numbers and influence have been in decline.

Liberal Republican Party: The Liberal Republicans of 1872 were a splinter party formed by reformers dissatisfied with the Grant administration, Reconstruction policy, and governmental corruption. Its presidential nominee, *New York Tribune* editor Andrew Greeley, was endorsed by the Democratic convention. However, many Democrats failed to support Greeley, a longtime critic of their party. The Liberal Republican party was weakly organized, underfinanced, and heavily dependent upon Democrats for support. It ceased to exist after 1872.

Libertarian Party: The libertarian doctrine asserts that individuals should be free to live their lives as they choose with a minimum amount of governmental intervention. They oppose laws that restrict basic civil liberties as well as restrictions on abortions, mandatory jury duty, the military draft, compulsory school attendance, minimum wage laws, and gun control legislation. Although it has built a nationwide organization and is financially viable, the party has not been able to build significant public support. As a minor party, its best showing was in 1980, when its nominee for president received over 1 million votes, but in 1996, its candidate received fewer than half that number (only .5 percent of the votes cast).

Liberty Party: This was the first American party formed on the basis of opposition to slavery in the 1830s. It had little electoral success, though it did spread and legitimize antislavery sentiment. The party ceased to exist after 1848, but one of its factions, led by Salmon P. Chase, helped to form the Free Soil party.

Nonpartisan League: The League was a potent political force in midwestern and western states during the 1916–1922 period. This agrarian radical movement was not a political party. Instead, it sought to exert influence by supporting candidates in primary elections. It retained its influence after the early 1920s in North Dakota, where it operated as a disciplined faction with the Republican party until the 1950s. It was taken over by young, liberal activists and the Farmers Union, who merged the league into the North Dakota Democratic party in 1956.

People's (Populist) Party: The Populist party was a part of the radical agrarian reform movement that swept across the West and South during the farm depression of the 1890s. The Populists advocated government ownership of railroads, free coinage of silver, an income tax, and an eight-hour work day. James Weaver, the party's 1892 presidential nominee, polled over 1 million votes and carried five states in the Midwest and West. When the forces of agrarian radicalism captured the Democratic party in 1896 and nominated William Jennings Bryan, the Populists endorsed Bryan, and most of their supporters entered the Democratic party.

Perot, H. Ross. The colorful and outspoken Texas billionaire ran as an independent candidate for president in 1992 mainly using his personal fortune to fund his campaign. Perot received 18.9 percent of the popular vote—the highest percentage of the vote won by an independent or third-party candidate since Theodore Roosevelt gained 27.5 percent as the Progressive nominee in 1912. For the 1996 campaign, he converted his United We Stand movement into a new party, the Reform party. His electoral support fell to 8.4 percent in 1996. After Republican conservative Pat Buchanan won the Reform party presidential nomination at the divisive 2000 convention, Perot endorsed Republican George W. Bush for president.

Progressive Party of 1924 (Robert M. La Follette): The Progressive party of 1924 was led by Wisconsin's Republican senator, Robert M. La Follette. La Follette sought to develop a party based upon labor and farmer support. He advocated government ownership of railroads and water power, protection of collective bargaining, direct primaries, and approval of wars by referendums. Although he received 16.6 percent of the vote, La Follette carried only his native state in the presidential election. His sons, Robert Jr. and Philip, formed the Progressive party of Wisconsin in the 1930s, and until 1946, this party was the principal opposition to the Republican party in the state.

Progressive Party of 1948 (Henry Wallace): One of the bases for the formation of the Progressive party was the unhappiness of the Democrats' left wing with Franklin Roosevelt's decision to drop Vice President Henry Wallace from the 1944 ticket in response to conservative pressures. After World War II, the left opposed President Truman's anticommunist policy of containment toward the Soviet Union and rallied around Wallace, who urged a more conciliatory policy toward the Communist bloc. Wallace also had support from Congress of Industrial Organizations (CIO) unions. As a presidential candidate, Wallace fared poorly, receiving only 2.4 percent of the vote.

Progressive Party of Wisconsin: In 1934, Senator Robert M. La Follette Jr. and his brother Philip led their followers out of the Wisconsin Republican party to form the Progressive party. This action was a culmination of a long struggle within the state GOP between the La Follettes' progressive faction and the conservative stalwarts. The La Follettes' Progressive party became the principal electoral opposition to the Republican party in the state. During the 1930s, the Progressives were able to elect Robert Jr. to the Senate and Philip to the governorship, while also winning control of the state legislature and House seats. However, the tides of national political alignments gradually swept over the state and strengthened the Democratic party at the expense of the Progressives during the early 1940s. Facing a difficult reelection battle in 1946, Robert La Follette Jr. chose to seek the Republican nomination for the Senate. He was defeated in the primary by Joseph McCarthy, and the Progressives disbanded as a separate party.

Reform Party: After losing as an independent candidate for president in 1992, H. Ross Perot used his ample resources to create a new Reform party. The party was essentially a personal vehicle for Perot, who proved to be a much less effective candidate in 1996 than he had been in 1992. However, by winning more than 5 percent of the popular vote in 1996, the Reform party qualified for $12.6 million in public funding in 2000. In 2000, the party was taken over by supporters of Pat Buchanan, the conservative television commentator and candidate for the Republican presidential nominations in 1992 and 1996. Amid internal divisiveness, right-wing campaign themes, and Perot's endorsement of Republican George W. Bush, the Reform party's share of the popular vote fell to only .42 percent in 2000, thereby losing any claim on public funding in 2004.

Socialist Party: Founded in 1901, the Socialist party was the only mass-based party of the left in the twentieth century. It achieved its greatest electoral strength during the pre–World War I era. Thus, in 1912, its presidential candidate, Eugene V. Debs, gained 6 percent of the popular vote. Its anti–World War I stance, suppression of its activities by the government, and internal splits over whether to adopt more radical and revolutionary tactics caused the party to go into decline. In addition, the Socialists were hurt by the absence of a strong sense of class consciousness in America.

Southern Democratic Party: The Southern Democratic party of 1860 was a transient third party formed as the Democratic party's northern and southern wings split in the midst of the pre–Civil War controversy over slavery. It nominated John C. Breckinridge, who carried the Deep South in the election. The party went out of business following the 1860 election and secession of the South from the Union.

States' Rights (Dixiecrat) Democratic Party: This was a splinter party composed of southern Democrats that formed following the adoption by the 1948 Democratic convention of a strong civil rights plank. The segregationist Dixiecrats selected Governor J. Strom Thurmond of South Carolina as their presidential nominee, who carried four Deep South states. There was no attempt by the Dixiecrats to organize a separate party that could run candidates for state offices. Instead, they worked within the Democratic parties of the southern states. Following the election, Thurmond and his supporters returned to the Democratic party.

Ventura, Jesse. The suburban Minneapolis mayor and former professional wrestler was the first Reform party candidate to be elected to a major office when he won the Minnesota gubernatorial election in a campaign that exploited his celebrity status, theatrics, tough-guy image, and antiestablishment populism. He defeated Hubert H. Humphrey III, the son of the state's most famous Democratic politician, and Norm Coleman, the Republican mayor of St. Paul. In 2000, Ventura left the Reform party after it nominated the former Republican conservative Pat Buchanan as its presidential nominee. He then formed the Minnesota Independence party, which competed in the 2000 elections but failed to elect any state or federal officials.

Notes

Chapter 1

1. Various political scientists have defined political parties in different ways. See Bibby, 2000, chap. 1; Maisel, 2001:10; Sorauf, 1980:17; Sartori, 1976:64; Epstein, 1980:9; Key, 1964:200; Downs, 1957:25; Neumann, 1956:356.

2. It should be noted here that the rules under which an election is run are very important in this regard. In New York state, for example, minor parties can endorse a major party candidate, and the candidate's votes on both party lines are added together to give his or her total. The result would be very different if the totals were counted separately, with the winner being the person with the most votes on one line. See Chapter 3.

Chapter 2

1. In all save two states (Maine and Nebraska), the winner of a plurality of the popular votes in any state wins all of that state's electoral votes. Thus, concentration of support in key states is needed to win electoral votes. See Chapter 3.

2. Since the 1980s, New York state politics has been further complicated by the presence of the Right-to-Life party, which endorses candidates solely based on their position on abortion. To date, it has not had the effect in statewide elections that the Liberals and Conservatives have had, but that potential remains possible.

Chapter 3

1. Each state has a number of electoral votes equal to the number of representatives (a function of population) plus senators (always two) that represent that state in the U.S. Congress. How those electoral votes are allocated within the state's total is determined by state law. Maine and Nebraska each award one electoral vote to the plurality winner in each congressional district within the state and two to the candidate with the plurality of votes for the entire state. Since these states have adopted this system, called the "district system," the same candidate has won each district and thus the entire state in each election, but this result is not inevitable.

Chapter 4

1. In 1974, Maine elected James Longley, running on the "Longley for ME" ticket, as governor. Longley defeated George Mitchell, who would later be elected to the U.S. Senate and serve as majority leader, and the state's Republican attorney general in that election. Longley seemed likely to win reelection in 1978 but decided not to seek a second term.

Third-party candidates have played an important role in each subsequent gubernatorial election and in a number of congressional and senatorial races. In 1992, Ross Perot received a higher percentage of the vote in Maine than in any other state; in fact, he finished second, ahead of President Bush. In the 1994 election won by King, the Green party candidate polled 6 percent of the vote; many feel that a majority of those votes would have gone to the Democrat, former governor and congressman Joseph Brennan, and would have given him a victory over King, had the Greens not been on the ballot.

2. It is interesting to note that Fasi ran as an independent candidate for governor in 1982, finishing second in that race as well.

3. Gubernatorial elections in thirty-six states were held in 1994 (and in 1998). Eleven states (including New Hampshire and Vermont, the only states that still elect governors for two-year terms) held elections for governor in 2000. Five states—Kentucky, Louisiana, and Mississippi in 1999 and New Jersey and Virginia in 2001—choose statewide officials in odd-numbered years.

4. The exact wording for the questions cited in this section can be found in Collet, 1996a:437–449.

5. The final results reveal the extent to which they failed. Republican candidates finished third in all three cases that we have mentioned in which independents won gubernatorial elections in this decade; the GOP candidate also finished third, behind the alternative candidate, in the Hawaii election won by the Democrat.

6. Interestingly, in 1996 Brennan and Collins were rematched in a U.S. Senate race to fill the seat vacated by Republican William Cohen. Again, third-party candidates played a role in the campaign. Collins beat Brennan by 31,601 votes, whereas the third-party candidates polled a total of 41,564 votes.

7. In the last two decades, only ten U.S. representatives and two senators have switched parties. The most prominent has been Phil Gramm (TX), who resigned the seat in the House he had won as a Democrat and then won a special election as a Republican, after having had a battle with Democratic House leadership over his alliance with the Republicans on budgetary matters, which had led to his removal from the Budget Committee. He went on to win a Senate seat and to compete for the presidential nomination as a Republican. None of the nine other representatives who switched gained much prominence in their new parties. In fact, three lost subsequent reelection bids. Of the senators who switched, both from Democrat to Republican, Richard Shelby (AL) and Ben Nighthorse Campbell (CO) won reelection in 1998. In addition, Harry Byrd (VA) left the Democratic party to become an independent, which he remained until his retirement.

8. Lamm did not decide to seek the Reform party nomination for president until after the efforts of the Gang of Seven collapsed.

9. Some caveats are in order: Carter has proven to be a remarkably popular former president; Humphrey was viewed as a stalwart in the Senate both before and after his years as vice president and his run for the presidency; Mondale was viewed as a strong vice president but a weak candidate; Dole's reputation in the Senate and as a war hero contrasted incredibly with his wooden image as a presidential campaigner.

Chapter 5

1. The procedure for the House resolving such contests is laid out in detail in Bibby, 2000, chap. 7; and Maisel, 2001, chap. 9.

2. In fairness to Wallace, it should be noted that he recanted many of his racist notions later in his life.

3. History is important here. Recall Chapter 2. Thurmond, in 1948, was the last third-party presidential candidate before Wallace to win any electoral votes. He did so by denying the Democratic candidate, President Harry Truman, southern electoral votes that at that time were all but assured for Democrats. Thurmond's issue was race, pure and simple. Thurmond lost that election but was elected to the U.S. Senate as a Democrat in 1954, the only senator ever to be elected on a write-in campaign. As he had promised, he resigned his seat and ran in a special election in 1956, to give South Carolinians a chance to vote for him directly. In his early Senate years, Thurmond was a staunch defender of racial segregation. In 1964, he switched from the Democratic to the Republican party, because the national Democratic party was under the control of liberals with whom he was uncomfortable. The Republicans promised that he could retain his seniority when he made that switch. Thurmond has always been a master politician. Although never reversing his conservative policy preferences, in 1971 he became the first southern Senator to hire an African American as a member of his professional staff. In 1996, Thurmond was reelected to the Senate, to begin serving his eighth term. Shortly after the 105th Congress convened, he became the longest-serving senator in American history; should he serve his full term, he will be 100 years old. (See Shaffer, 1991; Garson, 1974, Lachicotte, 1967.)

4. In stating that these problems should be addressed, we do not mean to diminish the difficulty of dealing with them. For instance, advertisements advocating particular views of public policy issues are exempt from regulation because they represent exactly the kind of free speech meant to be protected by the First Amendment to the Constitution. But a thin line separates those advertisements from others intended to impact on the result of an election by linking one candidate to a particular stance on an issue, often in an exaggerated (if not misleading) way. Similarly, closing the loopholes over soft money—money intended for party-building activities and not for a particular campaign for federal office (so-called hard money that must comply with more restrictive regulations)—can be done in a number of ways, each of which has different implications for the two political parties. Or providing free television for candidates seems a worthy goal, but resolving how to implement this reform, which candidates would be included, how much time would be provided, who would pay for the time, and similar questions requires a good deal of compromise and is much more difficult. We believe that the public would respond differently to real efforts at compromise as compared to obvious attempts to make political gains at the expense of the other party.

References

Abramson, Paul R., John H. Aldrich, Phil Paolino, and David W. Rohde. 2000. "Challenges to the American Two-Party System: Evidence from the 1968, 1980, 1992, and 1996 Presidential Elections." *Political Research Quarterly* 53:495–522.

_____. 1995. "Third-Party and Independent Candidates: Wallace, Anderson, and Perot." *Political Science Quarterly* 110:349–368.

Aldrich, John H. 1995. *Why Parties? The Origin and Transformation of Party Politics in America.* Chicago: University of Chicago Press.

Aldrich, John H., and Richard G. Niemi. 1996. "The Sixth American Party System." In *Broken Contract? Changing Relationships Between Americans and Their Government*, ed. Stephen C. Craig, 87–109. Boulder: Westview Press.

Ansolabehere, Stephen, and Alan Gerber. 1996. "The Effects of Filing Fees and Petition Requirements on U.S. House Elections." *Legislative Studies Quarterly* 21:249–264.

Ayres, Drummond Jr., and Michael Janofsky. 2000. "A Convention Ends Bitterly as It Began, with Rival Nominees and a Likely Lawsuit." *New York Times* (national edition), August 13–20.

Barone, Michael, and Grant Ujifusa. 1993. *The Almanac of American Politics, 1994.* Washington, DC: National Journal.

Bass, Harold. 1996. "Partisan Approaches to a Changing American Politics, 1946–1996: Partisan Institutions." Paper presented at the Annual Meeting of the American Political Science Association, San Francisco.

Beck, Paul Allen. 1997. *Party Politics in America.* 8th ed. New York: Longman.

Best, Judith. 1996. *The Choice of the People? Debating the Electoral College.* Lanham, MD: Rowman and Littlefield.

Bibby, John F. 2000. *Politics, Parties, and Elections in America.* 4th ed. Belmont, CA: Wadsworth.

Billington, Ray Allen. 1933. *The Protestant Crusade.* New York: Macmillan.

Brady, David W., and Kara Z. Buckley. 2002. "Governing by Coalition: Policymaking in the U.S. Congress." In *The Parties Respond*, 4th ed., ed. L. Sandy Maisel. Boulder: Westview Press.

_____. 1998. "Coalitions and Policy in the U.S. Congress: Lessons from the 103rd and 104th Congress." In *The Parties Respond*, 3d ed., ed. L. Sandy Maisel. Boulder: Westview Press.

_____. 1994. "Coalitions and Policy in the U.S. Congress." In *The Parties Respond*, 2d ed., ed. L. Sandy Maisel. Boulder: Westview Press.

Broder, David S. 1996. "The Party's Over: By 2000, the GOP or the Democrats Could Fade in Favor of a Third Party." *Washington Post*, August 11.

_____. 1980. *Pursuit of the Presidency.* New York: Berkeley Books.

Brogan, Dennis W. 1954. *Politics in America.* New York: Harper.

Burden, Barry C. 2001. "Did Ralph Nader Elect George W. Bush? An Analysis of Minor Parties in the 2000 Presidential Election." Paper presented at the Annual Meeting of the American Political Science Association, San Francisco, August 30–September 2.

Burnham, Walter Dean. 1970. *Critical Elections and the Mainsprings of American Politics.* New York: Norton.

Canfield, James Lewis. 1984. *A Case of Third-Party Activism.* Lanham, MD: University Press of America.

Collet, Christian. 2001. "Breaking Through? Minor Parties and the News Media in the 2000 Elections." Paper prepared for the "State of the Parties 2000 and Beyond" Conference sponsored by the Bliss Institute, University of Akron, October 18–20.

_____. 1997. "Taking the 'Abnormal' Route: Backgrounds, Beliefs, and Political Activities of Minor Party Candidates." In *Multiparty Politics in America*, ed. Paul S. Herrman and John C. Green. Lanham, MD: Rowman and Littlefield.

_____. 1996a. "Poll Trends: Third Parties and the Two Party System." *Public Opinion Quarterly* 60 (Fall):431–449.

_____. 1996b. "Minor Party Candidates in Sub-Presidential Elections: Backgrounds, Beliefs, and Political Activities." Paper presented at the Political Organizations and Parties Workshop on the Role of Third Parties, Annual Meeting of the American Political Science Association, San Francisco.

Cook, Rhodes. 1994. "Incumbent Advantage Lost in November." *Congressional Quarterly Weekly Report*, December 31.

_____. 1992. "House Republicans Scored a Quiet Victory in '92." *Congressional Quarterly Weekly Report*, November 10.

Downs, Anthony. 1957. *An Economic Theory of Democracy.* New York: Harper and Row.

Duverger, Maurice. 1963. *Political Parties.* New York: John Wiley and Sons.

Ehrenhalt, Alan. 1991. *The United States of Ambition: Power, Politics, and the Pursuit of Office.* New York: Times Books.

Eldersveld, Samuel J. 1964. *Political Parties: A Behavioral Analysis.* Chicago: Rand MacNally.

Epstein, Leon D. 1993. "Presidential Nominations Since Party Reform." *American Review of Politics* 14:149–162.

_____. 1986. *Political Parties in the American Mold.* Madison: University of Wisconsin Press.

_____. 1980. *Political Parties in Western Democracies.* New Brunswick: Transaction Publishers.

_____. 1967. *Political Parties in Western Democracies.* New York: Praeger.

Farnsworth, Clyde H. 1993. "Governing Tories in Canada Routed by Liberal Party." *New York Times*, October 26.

Fiorina, Morris. 1996. *Divided Government.* 2d ed. Boston: Allyn and Bacon.

Fischer, John. 1948. "Unwritten Rules of American Politics." *Harper's* 197 (November):27–36.

Garson, Robert. 1974. *The Democratic Party and the Politics of Sectionalism, 1941–1948.* Baton Rouge: Louisiana State University Press.

Gillespie, J. David. 1993. *Politics at the Periphery: Third Parties In Two-Party America*. Columbia: University of South Carolina Press.

Gimpel, James. 1996. *National Elections and the Autonomy of American State Politics*. Pittsburgh: University of Pittsburgh Press.

Gold, Howard J. 1995. "Third-Party Voting in Presidential Elections: A Study of Party, Anderson, and Wallace." *Political Research Quarterly* 48 (December):751–773.

Goldberg, Carey. 2000. "Vermont's 'Clean Money' Law Will Finance Underdog's Campaign." *New York Times* (national edition), June 15:A14.

Gray, Jerry. 1997. "The Budget Deal: The Overview; Bills to Balance the Budget and Cut Taxes Pass Senate." *New York Times*, August 1.

Greenhouse, Linda. 1997. "High Court Deals Setback to Minor Parties." *New York Times* (national edition), April 29.

Hames, Tim. 1997. "The Tactics That Triggered a Landslide." *London Times*, May 3.

Harmel, Robert. 1987. "New Parties and the Previous Party System: More of the Same or More Cracks in the Ice?" Paper presented at the Workshop on the Role of Small Parties, Joint Sessions of European Consortium for Political Research, Amsterdam, April 10–15.

Harmel, Robert, and John D. Robertson. 1985. "Formation and Success of New Parties: A Cross-National Analysis." *International Political Science Review* 6 (4):501–523.

Hazlett, Joseph M. II. 1992. *The Libertarian Party and Other Minor Political Parties in the United States*. Jefferson, NC: McFarland.

Holbrook, Thomas M. 1996. *Do Campaigns Matter?* Thousand Oaks, CA: Sage Publications.

Holt, Michael F. 1999. *The Rise and Fall of the Whig Party: Jacksonian Politics and the Onset of the Civil War*. New York: Oxford University Press.

Hosansky, David. 1997. "Scouting Out the Final Deal." *Congressional Quarterly Weekly Report* 55:1832.

Inglehart, Ronald. 1990. *Culture Shift in Advanced Industrial Democracies*. Princeton: Princeton University Press.

_____. 1987. "Value Change in Industrial Societies." *American Political Science Review* 81:1289–1303.

Janda, Kenneth. 1960. *Political Parties*. New York: Free Press

Jeter, Jon. 1998. "Campaign Reform Helped 'The Body' Olum Rivals." *Washington Post*, November 5:A41.

Just, Marion R. 1997. "Candidate Strategies and the Media Campaign." In *The Election of 1996: Reports and Interpretations*, ed. Gerald M. Pomper, 77–106. Chatham, NJ: Chatham House.

Keith, Bruce E., David B. Magleby, Candice J. Nelson, Elizabeth Orr, Mark C. Westlye, and Raymond E. Wolfinger. 1992. *The Myth of the Independent Voter*. Berkeley: University of California Press.

Kendall, Willmore, and Austin Ranney. 1956. *Democracy and the American Party System*. New York: Harcourt and Brace.

Key, V. O. Jr. 1964. *Politics, Parties, and Pressure Groups in America*. New York: Crowell.

_____. 1956. *American State Politics: An Introduction*. New York: Knopf.

_____. 1955. "A Theory of Critical Elections." *Journal of Politics* 17:3–18.

Klinkner, Philip A. 1996. *Midterm: The Elections of 1994 in Context.* Boulder: Westview Press.

Lachicotte, Alberta. 1967. *Rebel Senator, Strom Thurmond of South Carolina.* New York: Devin-Adair.

Ladd, Everett Carll. 1970. *American Political Parties: Social Change and Response.* New York: Norton.

Lentz, Jacob. 2002. *Electing Jesse Ventura: A Third Party Success Story.* Boulder: Lynne Rienner.

Lipset, Seymour Martin, and Stein Rokkan. 1967. *Party Systems and Voter Alignments: Cross-National Perspectives.* New York: Free Press.

Lowi, Theodore J. 1996. "Toward a Responsible Three-Party System: Prospects and Obstacles." In *The State of Parties: The Changing Role of Contemporary American Parties,* 2d ed., ed. John C. Green and Daniel M. Shea, 42–60. Lanham, MD: Rowman and Littlefield.

Maisel, L. Sandy. 2001. *Parties and Elections in America: The Electoral Process.* 3d ed., post-election update. Lanham, MD: Rowman and Littlefield.

_____. 1993. *Parties and Elections in America: The Electoral Process.* 2d ed. New York: McGraw-Hill.

Mann, Thomas E., and Norman J. Ornstein. 1994. *Congress, the Press, and the Public.* Washington: American Enterprise Institute and Brookings Institution.

"Many Americans Want Third Party Choice, No Matter Who the Nominees Are." 1999. Joan Shorenstein Center on the Press, Politics, and Public Policy, John F. Kennedy School of Government, Harvard University, December 21. Press Release.

Mayer, Kenneth R., and David T. Canon. 1999. *The Dysfunctional Congress: The Individual Roots of an Institutional Dilemma.* Boulder: Westview Press.

Mayhew, David. 1991. *Divided We Govern: Party Control, Lawmaking, and Institutions, 1946–1990.* New Haven: Yale University Press.

Mazmanian, Daniel. 1974. *Third Parties in Presidential Elections.* Washington, DC: Brookings Institution.

McCormick, Richard P. 1966. *The Second American Party System.* Chapel Hill: University of North Carolina Press.

Moore, David W. 2000. "Kick-Starting the Race: The Democratic Convention and Women Voters." *Public Perspective* (November/December):20–23.

_____. 1996. "The Party Really Isn't Over." *Public Perspective* (October/November):1–3.

Muller-Rommel, Ferdinand. 1990. *New Politics in Western Europe: The Rise and Success of Green Parties and Alternate Lists.* Boulder: Westview Press.

Muller-Rommel, Ferdinand, and Geoffrey Pridham, eds. 1991. *Small Parties in Western Europe: Comparative and National Perspectives.* Newbury Park, CA: Sage.

Nagourney, Adam. 1996. "Perot Chooses an Economist for His Ticket." *New York Times* (national edition), September 11.

Neto, Octavio Amorim, and Gary Cox. 1997. "Electoral Institutions, Cleavage Structure, and the Number of Parties." *American Journal of Political Science* 41:149–174.

Neumann, Sigmund, ed. 1956. *Modern Political Parties: Approaches to Comparative Politics.* Chicago: University of Chicago Press.

Partin, Randall W., Lori M. Weber, Robert B. Rapoport, and Walter J. Stone. 1994. "Sources of Activism in the 1992 Perot Campaign." In *The State of the Parties: The Changing Role of Contemporary American Parties*, ed. Daniel M. Shea and John C. Green, 147–162. Lanham, MD: Rowman and Littlefield.

Peltason, Jack W. 1999. "Constitutional Law for Political Parties." In *On Parties: Essays Honoring Austin Ranney*, ed. Nelson W. Polsby and Raymond E. Wolfinger, 9–42. Berkeley: Institue of Governmental Studies Press, University of California.

Penny, Timothy J., and Major Garrett. 1995. *Common Cents*. New York: Little, Brown.

Penny, Timothy J., and Steven C. Shier. 1996. *Payment Due: A Nation in Debt, a Generation in Trouble*. Boulder: Westview Press.

Polsby, Nelson W., and Aaron Wildavsky. 1996. *Presidential Elections: Strategies and Structures in American Politics*. 9th ed. Chatham, NJ: Chatham House.

Price, David E. 1984. *Bringing Back the Parties*. Washington, DC: CQ Press.

Rosenstone, Steven J., Roy L. Behr, and Edward H. Lazarus. 1996. *Third Parties in America*. 2d ed., rev. and exp. Princeton: Princeton University Press.

_____. 1984. *Third Parties in America: Citizen Response to Major Party Failure*. Rev. ed. Princeton: Princeton University Press.

Sartori, Giovanni. 1976. *Parties and Party Systems*. London: Cambridge University Press.

Scarrow, Howard. 1983. *Parties, Elections, and Representation in the State of New York*. New York: New York University Press.

Seelye, Katharine Q. 1997. "Parties Team Up to Protect Their Turf." *New York Times* (national edition), June 24.

Shaffer, Stephen D. 1991. "Strom Thurmond." In *Political Parties in the United States: An Encyclopedia*, ed. L. Sandy Maisel. New York: Garland.

Smallwood, Frank. 1983. *The Other Candidates: Third Parties in Presidential Elections*. Hanover, CT: Yale University Press.

Smith, Andrew E., Alfred J. Tuchfarber, Eric W. Rademacher, and Stephen E. Bennett. 1995. "Partisan Leaners Are Not Independents." *Public Perspective* (October/November):9–12.

Smith, Terrance. 1980. "Anderson's Long Race Against Long Odds." *New York Times*, October 4: sec. 1, 19.

Sorauf, Frank J. 1980. *Party Politics in America*. Boston: Little, Brown.

Stone, Walter J., and Ronald B. Rapoport. 2001. "It's Perot Stupid! The Legacy of the 1992 Perot Movement in the Major Party System, 1994–2000." *P.S. Political Science and Politics* 35:48–57.

Sundquist, James L. 1988. "Needed: A Political Theory for the New Era of Coalition Government in the United States." *Political Science Quarterly* 103:613.

_____. 1983. *Dynamics of the American Party System: Alignment and Realignment of Political Parties in the United States*. Rev. ed. Washington, DC: Brookings Institution.

"Third Party Sentiment Waxes and Wanes." 2000. *Public Perspective* (September/October):27.

"Washington Post Poll: Looking Ahead." 1998. *Washington Post*, December 27, A18.

"Win Your Way to Playoffs, Debate Chair Says." 2000. *Washington Post*, June 22, A6.

Winger, Richard. 1995. "How Ballot Access Laws Affect the U.S. Party System." *American Review of Politics* 16:321–351.

Index